TURDS OF GOLD

ALSO BY JUGAL MODY

Toke

TURDS OF GOLD

JUGAL MODY

HarperCollins *Publishers* India

First published in India by HarperCollins *Publishers* 2022
4th Floor, Tower A, Building No. 10, Phase II, DLF Cyber City,
Gurugram – 122002
www.harpercollins.co.in

2 4 6 8 10 9 7 5 3 1

Copyright © Jugal Mody 2022

P-ISBN: 978-93-5489-420-6
E-ISBN: 978-93-5489-421-3

This is a work of fiction and all characters and incidents described in this book are the product of the author's imagination. Any resemblance to actual persons, living or dead, is entirely coincidental.

Jugal Mody asserts the moral right
to be identified as the author of this work.

All rights reserved. No part of this publication may be reproduced, stored in a retrieval system, or transmitted, in any form or by any means, electronic, mechanical, photocopying, recording or otherwise, without the prior permission of the publishers.

Cover design: Paru Ramesh

Typeset in 11/15.2 Adobe Caslon Pro at
Manipal Digital Systems, Manipal

Printed and bound at
Thomson Press (India) Ltd

❋❋❋❋ HarperCollinsIn

This book is produced from independently certified FSC® paper
to ensure responsible forest management.

To Nayana Mody, Naresh Mody and Abhishek Mody

Dramatis Personae

The Gholte-Butala Family

Nikunj Gholte-Butala — Protagonist

Nikita Gholte-Butala — Digital Marketing champ and Nikunj's older sister

Vipulbhai Gholte — Assistant to Dr Garodia and Nikunj's father

Ilaben Gholte-Butala — Home chef and Nikunj's mother

Abhimanyu — Nikita's boyfriend

Nikunj's Friend Circle

Buzzcut — Beatmaker

Ghaps — Rapper

Raveena — Buzzcut's love interest and future manager of the friend circle

Utkarsha — Ghaps's love interest

Fehmida — TikTok influencer and Nikunj's love interest

The Sheths

Kalpeshbhai — Nikunj's client, who hasn't pooped in 20 years

Kashmira bhabhi — Kalpeshbhai's wife and primary caregiver

The Sheth Family — Owners of the nation's bestselling laxative, Param Churna

Dr Garodia's Clinic

Dr Garodia — Muscular Puncturopathy Therapist

Rameshbhai — Dr Garodia's devoted patient and deputy to Vipulbhai

Diksha bhabhi — Rameshbhai's wife and primary caregiver

The Picnic — Dr Garodia's waiting room, full of devoted patients

Nikunj's Caregiving Circle

Dhiraj — Nikunj's caregiving mentor, who later becomes his manager

Kapil Karmarkar — Disability rights activist, social worker, and Nikunj's client

Navinbhai, Dharmeshbhai, Prafuldada and others — Nikunj's clients

Ilaben's Circle of Influential Ladies

Shardaben — Ilaben's best friend and tiffin business partner

Toral bhabhi — Their younger, savvier neighbour who joins the tiffin business

Hansaben — Shardaben's elder sister and jhaad phook dabbler

Chhotiben — Shardaben's aunt and jhaad phook expert

Prologue

Dhiraj was rarely ever late, but on that day, he was. The highway was chock-a-block, as he weaved his way between cars, rickshaws, buses and trucks, riding his bike on dividers and footpaths, slipping in and out of the service lane, to ensure he somehow made up on lost time. His client, Dharmeshbhai of the famous Ghatkopar House of Gathiyas, wasn't the kindest soul and didn't mince words when it came to airing his grievances.

Dhiraj was a freelance caregiver, aka a half-nurse. People with disabilities and the elderly enlisted his services to help them perform their daily activities – from bathing to enemas to physiotherapy exercises. While Dharmeshbhai had been temporarily disabled due to a freak accident, his recovery had taken the longest because he refused to follow any of the instructions given by his doctors or take any of the medication prescribed.

Unfortunately for Dhiraj, he had to drive past Vile Parle to get to the Santacruz–Chembur Link Road on his way to Ghatkopar. The moment he passed the Bahar Cinema junction, and crossed the invisible border between Andheri and Vile Parle, he felt every last bit of water being drained from his body. His stomach caved in. His breakfast churned in his intestines, and bubbles of gas that tasted like deconstructed milk tea escaped his mouth in the form of a burp.

Dhiraj's elbows fell weak and he hit the brakes before he could hurt himself. Breathless and drenched in sweat, he felt all the undigested food in his stomach make a beeline for his anus. He dropped his bike sideways, and tried to recompose himself. He looked at his watch, and cursed his wife for not checking if the milk had gone bad before making tea with it.

To his surprise, a lot of the vehicles around him were pulling over, and their occupants falling out of their car seats on to the side of the highway. Some curled up in a foetal position. Others screamed in the vain hope of finding a bathroom to use.

Finally settling into this unsettled state, Dhiraj picked his bike up and continued riding till he reached the airport junction, which was full of hotels and a couple of public toilets – all of which had long lines snaking outside them already. Finally, he gave up on decency, sneaked into the ruins of Jas Hotel, the one abandoned hotel and relieved himself. He looked at his watch to see that it was already time for his appointment. His phone started ringing and flashing Dharmeshbhai's name and face. He ignored the call because he was, nonetheless, going to get an earful when he got there. Why take the call and be told off, he reasoned to himself.

Someone from another dark corner of the ruins shouted, 'SHUT YOUR PHONE! I CAN'T GO!'

Maybe the news channels were not lying. They had said that an unknown loose motion epidemic had suddenly hit the people of Vile Parle. The week before, it had been Grant Road and gas, and the week before that it had been Chinchpokli and constipation. Most people didn't take it seriously till it hit their area.

When Dhiraj felt he had no more to add to the ruins of the long-forgotten Jas Hotel, he pulled out the wet wipes he always carried with him for his clients. He shouted, 'Best of luck!' to the man in the other corner, and got back on his bike to get to Ghatkopar. On his way, he stopped by a zunka bhakar centre to grab a nimbu pani to rehydrate. His completely empty stomach felt unsettled with nausea and exhaustion. As soon as Dhiraj crossed the next signal and entered Santacruz, his stomach felt fine again. Like none of what had transpired in the last half an hour – which felt like many hours ago now – had happened at all.

That was the moment Dhiraj knew that whatever was affecting the city of Mumbai, everything that he had been ignoring in the news, was not natural. He remembered the stories his guru had told him: Of Tatti Raja, a superhealer, who could make anybody poop on command and, with that poop, heal any stomach illness that person had.

Dhiraj prayed for the arrival of Tatti Raja.

1

A gastric epidemic was affecting the stomachs of Mumbai like it was playing an idle tap mobile game on a map of the city. It was an epidemic made of many small epidemics, ranging from constipation to loose motion. It affected a suburb – and every house there would have at least one infected person – for a few weeks, and then moved on to the next. The government had no idea what had hit the city. None of the food and water tests showed anything abnormal. The germ levels were, as they always were, a little higher than the healthy limit.

Mulund had so far escaped the wrath of the tummy troubles. Nikunj Gholte-Butala had lived all his life in the Gujarati part of this Central Line suburb, in a 1BHK, a lane away from the lane famous for having the highest number of farsan shops in the city. Oil fumes always hung low over the street from the constant frying and consumption of snacks.

Nikunj had just finished his BA from one of those colleges with a really long name. Being the younger of two siblings, and the only son, he wasn't expected to contribute financially (or otherwise) to the family till he got a job. Nikunj still didn't know what he planned to do with his life once the summer of 2018 was over and he got his BA final year results. His worst-case scenario was to apply for a loan, buy a bike and work for one of the food delivery apps or runner services. He could always join his uncle's farsan shop, but he didn't want to because, one, it was all the way in Kandivali and, two, farsan wasn't really his thing (tandoori chicken and anda bhurji were more his jam). He couldn't join his other uncle's accountancy practice because he was an Arts student.

Nikunj wondered what direction his life would take once the results came out. His classmates joked about how this would be the last vacation of their lives. Some had even made TikTok videos, shooting themselves in slow motion. Others had already gotten jobs in offices, where someone from their family worked, or at their father's shops, or taken up economy gigs. Three classmates joined small digital agencies as actual paid interns. One classmate joined an animal rights NGO, and another joined a Mulund-based cable news and infotainment channel. The only ones left were Buzzcut, Ghaps (short for Ghapaghap) and Nikunj, who were a group on WhatsApp, on the last bench of their class, and in real life.

The whole 'last-vacation-ever' business got to their heads. So Buzzcut, Ghaps and Nikunj decided to make it the most vela summer of their lives. The three of them pooled in Rs 2000 and bought 100 grams of weed. Every afternoon, Ghaps stole three bottles of beer from her family's wine shop, and met Buzzcut and Nikunj in the garden on one corner of the neighbourhood maidan. While everyone else played cricket, the trio sat under a tree in a corner and proceeded to get bombed. Twice, they rode triples on Buzzcut's bike and went to a resort in Virar, via Ghodbunder Road. The resort gave them an AC room and access to the pool for the day for 500 bucks. They pooled in the petrol money and ate at the food stalls on the beach outside the resort.

True to his name, Buzzcut had a buzzcut. Every week or two, when his hair grew out, he changed the inscription on the buzzed part of the cut. His hair art always had the motif of a lightning bolt. Buzzcut always wore a hoodie (with the hood off), no matter how hot it got in summer. And to go with the hoodies, Buzzcut had two pairs of jeans and one pair of cargo pants.

Ghaps's real name was Gayatri Kumar. She was damn pissed about it. Only aunties were called Gayatri, she said. Larger than life and with something to say about everything, Ghaps always wore a colourful cotton Indian-style skirt with a bright shirt or a T-shirt with some catchphrase printed on it. She always had clip-on piercings on her face and earrings, which she removed only when she slept. She had given herself the nickname 'Ghapaghap' because when she was hungry, she ate pani puri ghapaghap, when she was drinking, she did shots ghapaghap, and when she rapped, she 'put rhyme on rhyme ghapaghap, bachi!' When she spoke, she even cussed ghapaghap.

Ghaps's rhymes were always accompanied by Buzzcut's beats. But she still hadn't had the chance to showcase talent of rapping, cussing, cussing while rapping, and rapping while cussing anywhere outside of Instagram. Secretly, both Buzzcut and Nikunj knew, she was afraid to try because she was afraid she would fail. Instagram and YouTube were safe spaces because then you always had a ready excuse: 'I've just not been discovered yet.'

That day, Ghaps had stolen six bottles of beer. 'Aaj Saturday hai and Saturdays should have more chill in them.'

Buzzcut, whose bag was their official weed storage unit, agreed. 'Toh aaj, we double the number of joints too.' He pulled out two fat kalis instead of one.

After six joints and six bottles of beer, the three of them were successfully swimming in a place just outside reality. That's when Ghaps's phone dinged. She picked it up to see a notification from their one and only fan: Utkarsha.

'Bachi! This Utkarsha chick is really into our sound, isn't she?'

'Or she's into one of you?' said Nikunj.

'Band bana nahi, Yoko pehle aa gayi?' Buzzcut laughed even though he was actually afraid of Utkarsha turning into their Yoko.

'What if I have sex with her and then realize that I don't love her?' Ghaps had other imaginary problems. 'I don't want any chick drama.'

'You're a chick.' Buzzcut laughed.

'But I'm a ghapaghap chick, bachi. Not like other chicks.' Ghaps pushed him. 'You say no, has Raveena even said Hi to you?'

Buzzcut's college crush, Raveena, lived two lanes away from his house. He sometimes took the longer route to his house to see if they would still acknowledge each other if they ran into one another.

'I've passed her twice and we have only waved at each other so far.' Buzzcut took a sip of his beer.

Nikunj, of course, didn't tell them that he had been chatting up Fehmida on Instagram (@ghalatfehmida). By chatting up, he meant he sent her a 'Hi', and she'd reply with a 'Hi' and a link to her latest TikTok (for Nikunj to heart). Then she'd ask him to send her a selfie. It was like Nikunj and Fehmida were in Prolonged Eye-Contact 2.0.

Fehmida's eyes always pierced Nikunj's soul. He wanted to believe that she must have been using enchanted kohl. The only jewellery she wore were earrings and a silver nose ring with a diamond flashing in it. Fehmida was always dressed in tight jeans and flat shoes.

Nikunj hadn't told Ghaps and Buzzcut about Fehmida because he didn't want them making fun of her grin. It was a liberated and post-ironic grin, with all her teeth on display. Nikunj knew that Buzzcut and Ghaps would call her 'faavda bhabhi', and he would get pissed and scream at them. Then Buzzcut and Ghaps would apologize after a couple of days. And then Nikunj would have to forgive them in a dramatic and quiet Bharat-milaap scene. Nikunj didn't want any of that drama. Plus, Fehmida and him had just started talking. That didn't mean anything.

So that Saturday evening, as the last two cricket teams were packing their gear and making their way to the golawala outside the maidan, Buzzcut, Ghaps and Nikunj pulled their phones out to play some PUBG. That was when Nikunj's sister Nikita called.

He pulled himself out of the stupor, picked his phone up and sounded sober as ever.

There were no hi's or hello's. 'Where are you? Listen carefully. Papa has had a stroke at Dr Garodia's clinic." Nikita said each word very deliberately. "Come to the clinic. They have called an ambulance for him. Aai is on her way to the clinic. I will meet both of you at the hospital. You got it?'

'Yes.' Nikunj knew better than to ask questions.

His high immediately took a backseat. He turned to Buzzcut and Ghaps, and the look on his face told them everything they needed to know. The three of them took a rickshaw to the clinic.

2

Nikunj's father, Vipulbhai, was in the AC cabin of Dr Garodia's clinic when a clot in his bloodstream reached his brain. He clutched his head and collapsed on to the floor, pushing against the wheelchair in the room, which rolled across the floor and slammed straight into Dr Garodia's crotch.

Dr Garodia stopped himself from screaming, walked out of the cabin into the waiting area of the clinic, and announced the collapse of his assistant to his patients. Then, he spread his arms wide and said, 'I am going to revive him with my powers.' He invited the accompanying relatives of four of his patients to help him prop Vipulbhai up on the executive chair. Dr Garodia pressed the muscular puncturopathy points with his fingers as the AC inside cooled down the waiting room outside. The chill breeze coming through the door hypnotized the sweat-drenched audience.

Five minutes into the show, the aunty who always wore a Punjabi suit and Keds panicked. She had seen this before with her father. He had had a stroke and died in front of her eyes. She sprung to action, calling an ambulance, and then finding Vipulbhai's phone and contacting his wife, Ilaben, with it. Most of the others thought of her as a heretic, a philistine, to not have enough faith in Dr Garodia and his muscular puncturopathy.

Vipulbhai had been an assistant to Dr Garodia, the famous 'muscular puncturopathy' therapist, for almost six years. Don't bother googling muscular puncturopathy therapy. Dr Garodia had entirely made it up. And he kept building on his tale to change any circumstance in his favour. Nobody knew what Dr Garodia's real education was. He claimed that he knew specific points of energy in the human body, which, when punctured by his fingers, and his fingers only, could heal any disease or disability. According to him, one was chosen to be a muscular puncturopathist by the universe; you couldn't just become a muscular puncturopathist, even if you studied it extensively.

Ghaps, Buzzcut and Nikunj arrived at the clinic just as the ambulance was pulling in. The ward boys and the real doctor jumped out of the ambulance and ran to the cabin. Dr Garodia welcomed them warmly, and moved aside to let them do their work. He noticed that he was losing his patients' attention to the work of a real doctor. So he quickly told the real doctor, 'I have him ready for you. I have applied pressure to the right muscular puncturopathy points in his body. Your job should be easy from here on.'

The real doctor ignored him and looked around the room till he spotted Nikunj, who resembled his father. 'Are you his son? We have to take him to the hospital urgently.'

Swimming as his head was, Nikunj just nodded.

'Move aside then.'

The ward boys brought in the stretcher and transferred Vipulbhai on to it. As they carried him to the ambulance, Nikunj's mother, Ilaben, reached the clinic. Nikunj ushered her straight from her rickshaw into the ambulance with Vipulbhai. Buzzcut and Ghaps decided to wait at the clinic in case Nikita got there. Nikita, who was still on her way, messaged Nikunj urgently: 'Keep all the bills and paperwork from the hospital. My office's health insurance plan will cover this.'

After the procedure, Vipulbhai did not wake up until the next morning. Various members from their extended family and friends from Bhayandar and Mira Road, arrived late that night and stayed with the family outside the hospital. Almost everyone Vipulbhai was related to by blood or through work showed up. In his community, he was known as the family member with the most experience of hospitals. If anyone in his circle needed to be hospitalized, they would call him. He would make a list of things to pack and an itinerary to follow, and then he would be there himself to help. So when Vipulbhai was admitted to the hospital, the news spread like wildfire and everyone showed up with food, a bag (each) filled with Vipulbhai's list of hospital things, and wads of cash.

Ilaben borrowed some cash from her brother. For the most part, they used Nikita's two credit cards – both of which had been kept aside to use only for emergencies. The next day, Nikita took Nikunj with her to the bank to break some FDs and withdraw cash. The feeling of being alone inside a hustling and bustling bank branch was the first time Nikunj felt financial anxiety. The standing in line, the filling of forms, the wait, the look from the cashier (like he didn't really want to give away the money) – everything made Nikunj feel that losing this much money must be a big deal.

The day after Vipulbhai regained consciousness, both Nikita and Ilaben returned to their jobs. Ilaben had recently scaled-up her small tiffin business. She had expanded from providing tiffin service to people in their building complex to the entire neighbourhood.

Nikita, on the other hand, had completed her BMM and landed herself a well-paying job as a junior account manager at GloboKon, a big multinational digital agency. When she was still in college, she would help her mother in the morning with the cooking for the tiffins. After Nikita started working, Shardaben entered the lives of the Gholte-Butalas. Shardaben lived next door and had just sent her only son to the US. She suddenly realized that she had a lot more time on her hands than she thought she would. So she and Ilaben started working together, and expanded the business some more. For the first day of Vipulbhai's hospitalization, Shardaben managed the entire cooking by herself.

That day onwards, the responsibility of taking care of Vipulbhai fell on Nikunj by default. Obviously, the women couldn't stop working. Vipulbhai, of course, didn't want to stay at the hospital at all. 'These doctors don't know what they are doing. Take me to Dr Garodia, and I will be fine in no time.' Once every few hours, he threw a tantrum, tried to get up, pack his bag, and asked the nurse to do his final billing.

The nurses just made excuses and vanished until the doctor showed up for rounds. Or until Ilaben or Nikita showed up to give Vipulbhai stern looks.

The problem was Vipulbhai had still not regained the use of many parts of his body. His left eyelid drooped a little. His eyes didn't respond fast enough to the doctors shining a torch into it. He didn't have complete control over his hands. They sometimes didn't move at all.

By the time Vipulbhai got discharged, he was mostly alright. Except for his eyes and hands. His fingers didn't respond to signals from his brain. And he had to wear sunglasses all the time. (Nikunj magnanimously lent his father his old pair of reflective aviators, which he hadn't worn since they went out of style.) The doctors said it would take some time and physiotherapy for things to return to normal.

Vipulbhai scoffed. 'Dr Garodia will fix it in no time,' he declared. Nikunj was highly embarrassed by his father's ungrateful behaviour. But the doctors didn't mind. They were used to having alternative medicine bhakts as patients. So they just smiled, listened to their beliefs, and later laughed at the stories during tea breaks.

3

Once Vipulbhai was discharged, Nikunj and his father became regulars at the waiting area of Dr Garodia's clinic. Dr Garodia's clinic used to be an old real estate office. The walls still had frames with printouts of architectural designs and building projects. The clinic was in a lane with only hardware shops, one dairy and an old single-screen theatre (which played only Bhojpuri films since the multiplexes invaded). The real estate office belonged to one of Dr Garodia's patients, who had been cured of his sciatica – which was one of few things that Dr Garodia had often successfully cured. That, spondylitis and slipped discs were his forte.

The AC cabin of the real estate office, where Vipulbhai had had his stroke, was Dr Garodia's consultation room. The outer non-AC part of the office was the designated waiting area. The furniture had all been moved along the walls, and various patients were parked on it. The waiting area was always filled with people. Some of the regulars had chronic illnesses or disabilities, and had been coming to Dr Garodia for over five years, hoping for a miracle cure. They would come with their tiffin boxes and wait for hours. Some stayed behind even after their session. Over the years, they had all become friends and extended family for one another. The clinic had come to resemble a family picnic. Sometimes, they also conducted business deals in the waiting area. Then there was the WhatsApp version of pop-up shops. Some of the picnic members used it to sell small trinkets (like bootlegged Disney keychains and mugs), health products, fake Tupperware and cheap electronics.

Vipulbhai, who was used to being the inside man, found it a little difficult to accept his new place in the waiting area. On his first day in the waiting area, all the other patients came up to him and wished him a speedy recovery. According to what became the legend, Vipulbhai's life was only saved because he had the stroke under Dr Garodia's chhatrochhaya. Dr Garodia was able to repair him enough to make it easy for the hospital doctors to then save him. If Vipulbhai had had a stroke at his own home, he might have never recovered. And Vipulbhai soon began repeating this story to everyone who would hear; of how Dr Garodia had fought the stroke and saved his life.

Nikunj did not have to worry about finding a job any time soon. His life's first job was to take care of Vipulbhai, while Nikita and Ilaben ran the house. There was obviously a gap in the family income, which meant the Gholte-Butalas' monthly savings had reduced by half. Sometimes, Nikunj didn't know what had hit him. One day, he was getting stoned and drunk with Ghaps and Buzzcut, and the next, he was following Vipulbhai around the house. Since his father couldn't use his hands, he depended on Nikunj for everything – from shit to shower. Nikunj not only had to help him undo his pants, but also ensure his pee didn't miss the pot.

According to Dr Garodia, Vipulbhai did not just have a muscular problem but also a neurological problem. Such a complex problem would need the help of some kaadhaas. By the end of that week, Nikunj's duties involved making three different types of kaadhaas for Vipulbhai, for his nerves and brain to heal from the stroke. All of this cost money, and had started eating into the family's savings. Of course, Vipulbhai also had to buy faafda and jalebi for everyone at the clinic. Snacks were a waiting area tradition—everyone got some food; usually what they or some shop in their area were famous for. Three months in, Vipulbhai's expenditures started annoying Ilaben a little.

The only time Nikunj got to blow off some steam was late at night. After Ilaben and Vipulbhai went to sleep, Nikunj would meet Ghaps and Buzzcut, and get stoned. From them he learnt that Ghaps had started talking to Utkarsha on Instagram. And Raveena and Buzzcut had still not moved past waving to one another.

Meanwhile, Fehmida who had just captained a switch of platforms in their relationship from Instagram to WhatsApp had stopped responding to Nikunj's messages on WhatsApp. She only sent him TikTok and Instagram links to heart, while he continued to grovel for forgiveness. The reason for this snub was a WhatsApp meme that Nikunj had forwarded to Fehmida. It had a screenshot from the famous old Liril ad, with a half-naked girl under a waterfall. 'This ad sets unrealistic expectations for women,' it declared on top. And then added at the bottom, 'There can't be a waterfall in the kitchen.'

One night, after getting stoned with Ghaps and Buzzcut, Nikunj collapsed in the living room sofa, and switched on the TV. He and Nikita slept in the living room, while Vipulbhai and Ilaben slept in the bedroom. Once they went into their room and changed, they didn't come out till the morning.

Nikunj was watching a long news report on the constipation wave in Santacruz (more than fifty thousand people claimed to have had constipation for almost a week) when Nikita came home drunk from an office party.

She collapsed next to Nikunj and shouted, 'Get me some water! Why are you just sitting around so lazily?'

Nikita had been very irritable with Nikunj of late. Nikunj quietly got up to get her some water. Halfway into the glass, Nikita started crying. 'I'm sorry,' she whispered. 'I know how much you're doing around the house these days. I didn't mean what I said.'

'I know,' said Nikunj.

'You know, you have to be like takatak cool when you work in a big office.'

'Mhanje?'

'Like when you talk, you not only have to impress people with your ideas but by the words you use to describe them and how you pronounce those words.' Nikita's accent was half-American because of *Friends* and half-Mulund because of, well, Mulund.

Nikunj understood what she was saying but that had never been a problem for him. His friends, classmates and even his college professors, spoke English approximately.

'They don't even call me for cigarette breaks. I mean, I also smoke. I can also – *heeheehee* – laugh at your jokes.'

It wasn't that Nikita wasn't great at her job and didn't receive constant attention and praise from senior management. There was just an invisible wall that she couldn't surmount. And then there was the ticking bomb at home that was weighing on Nikita's mind.

'Papa needs to accept certain things and move on. This whole waiting for a miracle to happen is burning a hole in all that Aai and I have built.'

'I'll start looking for a job.' Nikunj suddenly realized he wasn't sure if he would be able to find a job if he tried. He considered working for Dr Garodia as Vipulbhai's replacement, but somebody else had already volunteered for the assistant gig. This one worked for free, purely out of his devotion to Dr Garodia. He was a relative of one of the patients (the patient still didn't get any discount, though).

'That you will, but then who will take care of Papa?'

'Something will work out. Dr Garodia is saying that he is very close to curing Papa and his fingers will start working again. Then in the next six months, he will fix his eyes.'

'That's too long. I don't think Dr Garodia will be able to cure anything. Papa needs to go to his physiotherapy sessions.' Just hearing Dr Garodia's name made Nikita angry. Just like it always made Ilaben mad. The two women never talked about this in front of Vipulbhai or Nikunj though. Nikunj had only once overheard them making snide comments about Dr Garodia. Nikita was a woman of science, and Ilaben was more invested in mythology than science. But together, they hated how much faith Vipulbhai had in Dr Garodia to continue working for him.

'I am serious, Niku. We all know that the only success stories we have heard from Dr Garodia's clinic are of sciatica, spondylitis and slipped disc.'

Nikunj hated going to the clinic with Vipulbhai because of the 'picnics' in the waiting area. It was just endless chapad-chapad and chow-chow. He hated the endless devoutness that everyone at the picnic, including Vipulbhai, had for Dr Garodia. Nikunj wondered if he was just envious of Dr Garodia's godliness. This was the first time that Nikita expressed her anger about him so openly in front of Nikunj (he wondered how drunk she was to have said these things).

'I know. I'll talk to Papa and take him to physiotherapy once,' he mused out loud. 'Maybe if he feels that it is doing something for his condition, he will go back for a second sitting.'

'Yes, maybe. You don't worry about taking up a job right now. Take care of Papa; we'll talk about it in a month again.'

An hour after Nikita crashed, Vipulbhai gave Nikunj a missed call. That was their late-night signal for Nikunj to meet Vipulbhai outside the bathroom. As Nikunj helped him pee, he told his father, 'We're going to take an appointment with a physiotherapist tomorrow.'

With Vipulbhai's pants down in the middle of the night, it was the only time Nikunj could have made this suggestion. Any other time of the day, Vipulbhai would've definitely thrown a tantrum. At night, he had too much dignity to dare and wake up Ilaben or Nikita from their night's sleep after a full day's work.

4

Later that week, Nikunj and Vipulbhai went to the physiotherapist. On the way, Vipulbhai called Dr Garodia and apologized for missing the appointment and blamed Nikunj for forcing him. Dr Garodia patiently listened to all the apologies and then told Vipulbhai to come after the physiotherapy appointment. He said, 'That is the least I can do after the years you have given in my service.'

Nikunj was okay with being thrown under the bus. He knew he would get some grief from Dr Garodia the next time he saw him. In fact, the doctor would do that thing that uncles always do when they feel like they've been outsmarted – try and act smarter with a hint of 'see what I'm going to do now'. Not that they ever did anything, but the posturing was necessary for their ego.

After the Dr Garodia call, Vipulbhai called Rameshbhai in the waiting area, and asked him to pass the phone around. At first, neither side could hear the other properly because Vipulbhai's rickshaw was stuck in a traffic jam and everybody was fighting with their horns. So Vipulbhai, as well as the patients, started screaming on both ends of the phone. Vipulbhai apologized to every picnic member, including a new patient (whom he had never met before), for not making it to the clinic that day with snacks.

And once they reached the physiotherapy clinic, Vipulbhai refused to cooperate, while Nikunj did everything he could to get his father to follow the physiotherapist's instructions. But Vipulbhai just sat there – stewing in his refusal to cooperate, like a gharelu Madhubala, hands drooping and looking away from the therapist. Meanwhile, Vipulbhai's inner voice chanted to maintain his balance: 'Jai Shri Dr Garodia-ae-oh Namaha.' Because Vipulbhai had launched a non-cooperation movement, Nikunj had to note down all the exercises the therapist was making him do. He knew that the duties of making his father do the exercises at home till the next appointment would fall on him.

From the physiotherapy centre, Vipulbhai directed their rickshaw to go straight to Dr Garodia's. When Dr Garodia was treating Vipulbhai, Vipulbhai wouldn't stop apologizing for Nikunj. Dr Garodia feigned humility and said, 'Don't embarrass me, Vipulbhai. We are like family only.' Then he looked at Nikunj. 'Vipulbhai, you have heard that Kalavati story from the stories of Satyanarayan?'

'The one where Sadhu forgets to perform the Satyanarayan puja?'

'And how much pain Kalavati's husband had to go through? You have to have faith, Vipulbhai. Our younger generation will never understand this.'

Nikunj brushed off his behaviour.

Later that night, over dinner, Nikunj grabbed the opportunity to diss Dr Garodia in front of an audience that would care. And Vipulbhai couldn't say anything because Nikunj was the one feeding him and made sure his mouth was full at the right times.

'Maney khabar nathi tamne enama bhagwan kem dekhaay chhe!' began Nikunj, and Ilaben froze, mid-chew. 'I sometimes feel bad that all those people who gather there with all that food, and are just wasting their time instead of finding real help. I am here trying to help you, but no you want to listen to that man who, instead of encouraging you to go to physiotherapy, is taunting me!'

Even Nikita, who always watched TV during their dinners, had switched it off, and was listening to Nikunj.

'Bilkul! Pela divsay, he was saying Dr Garodia's name in his sleep!' chimed in Ilaben, who had finally been given a chance to air her grievances against the doctor. 'Sansar thi mukti toh bas Dr Garodia na sharan maaj chhe, kem? In a day, he utters Dr Garodia's name more times than mine or even God's. Atli vaar bhagwan nu naam lidhu hoat toh ae pan prakat thai gaya hot.'

'Papa, I am warning you!' said Nikita firmly, as she mopped up the last bit of sabzi on her plate with the last bit of chapati. 'If because of Dr Garodia, you stop going to physiotherapy, toh maara thhi kharab koi nai thaay!'

Ilaben and Nikunj exchanged a quick glance as the chapatti hotbox made space for the rice tapeli on their small foldable dining table. Both of them agreed that they had bullied their disabled husband and father a bit too much. Nikita, however, continued as the other three ate in complete silence.

'How much money do you pay him daily for this fake treatment? I have a better idea, why don't you make paper planes out of the currency notes and shoot them out on to the streets? At least koi gareeb ne malshe toh he will bless you and that blessing might actually cure you!'

But all their words fell on mostly deaf ears. Vipulbhai's devotion was unsullied. The next day, after Nikunj helped Vipulbhai with his bath, the two sat down in the living room. Nikunj began guiding his father through the physiotherapy exercises, but Vipulbhai's non-cooperation movement continued. He looked away as Nikunj performed the exercises using his fingers and wrists. Every now and then, he would sigh loudly and dramatically in protest.

This went on for a few days. On the fourth day, Vipulbhai came out of the toilet and announced that physiotherapy had given him constipation. 'In my fifty-six years, I have never had constipation. I start physiotherapy for four days, and it happens!'

Ilaben and Nikunj tried to convince him otherwise, but this Madhubala wouldn't relent. So the family decided to divert their attention to fixing Vipulbhai's bowel movements. They tried everything from haritaki to isabgol, Param Churna to allopathic laxatives, but nothing worked. It was like Vipulbhai's stomach was hoarding food and laxatives that could power their neighbourhood with biogas for a decade. Vipulbhai's paunch had started to look like a balloon.

———✹———

On the fifth day, Vipulbhai flat out refused to even watch Nikunj do his physiotherapy exercises for him. Ilaben and

Nikunj chased him around the living room. But he darted towards the door, put on his chappals and walked out of the house by himself. Nikunj couldn't run behind him because he was wearing only his boxers and no T-shirt. Ilaben couldn't chase after Vipulbhai because she had to return to the kitchen to finish all the cooking for her tiffin service. (While all of this was happening, Shardaben was in the Gholte-Butala kitchen, peeling lauki and listening to a Bhagwat Saptaah on the Bluetooth speaker she had bought online for Rs 200.)

'Don't worry. Mullah ni daud masjid tak… He will be at Dr Garodia's clinic. Go put on some clothes.' Ilaben pulled out a 200-rupee note from her kitchen purse and handed it to Nikunj. And she was right. Vipulbhai had taken a rickshaw and stopped at the farsan shop on his way to the clinic. He asked the shop boys to load the rickshaw with faafda–jalebi and take the money from his shirt pocket. At the clinic, other regulars helped unload him and the faafda–jalebi off the rickshaw. They even paid for the auto without Vipulbhai having to ask.

By the time Nikunj got there, his father was already in the AC cabin getting his treatment. Dr Garodia recognized the opportunity he had when he found out that Vipulbhai had come alone. Nikunj waited out in the waiting area for fifteen minutes, hoping that, at some point, Vipulbhai or Dr Garodia would call him in. But they didn't. When Nikunj finally burst into the AC cabin unannounced, Dr Garodia looked up from the newspaper he was reading. Vipulbhai was nowhere to be seen. Then, suddenly, the attached toilet's door was kicked open. Vipulbhai stepped out. His face lit the room up with the dazzling warmth of the winter sun. 'Param Anand!' he said before he walked to Dr Garodia, pressed his upper body against Dr Garodia's, and rested the side of his head on his huge chest. The moment was very reminiscent of the Sudama-Krishna embrace. 'Thank you, doctor! I am all clear!'

'Arre! What are you saying, sir ji! I can cure HIV also with muscular puncturopathy therapy. If only some people have faith.' He gave Nikunj a sly look as he said this.

'You see?' Vipulbhai turned to Nikunj. 'Physiotherapy gave me constipation, and Dr Garodia removed it. You still think I should do physiotherapy instead of coming to Dr Garodia? For five days, I couldn't take a good tatti!'

Nikunj just sighed. 'Okay, okay. Aai must be worried, let's go home.'

That night, over dinner, Vipulbhai didn't eat a morsel. Instead, he chose to make an impassioned speech to an audience of Nikita, Ilaben and Nikunj. Nikunj held a morsel in front of Vipulbhai's face for a few minutes, but when Vipulbhai wouldn't stop talking, he put the food back on his plate. Nikunj pretended to listen to his father, whereas Nikita and Ilaben had given up all pretence. They were openly facing the TV, set to *Yeh Rishta Anokha*, far more interested in seeing whether the mother-in-law would successfully turn the family against the elder daughter-in-law because she forgot to put kesar in the kheer.

Meanwhile, Vipulbhai was on a filibuster. He renounced all other forms of medical practice, and swore an oath to muscular puncturopathy therapy. 'Even in the West, white people are turning to alternative medicine. We toh have grown up with alternative medicine all around us.' Then he proceeded to narrate the story of how Dr Garodia earned a degree after going to the secret muscular puncturopathy school in Germany for the ones chosen by the universe. When he paused and asked Nikunj to give him a sip of water, Nikita looked away from her plate and the TV for the first time in the entire course of the dinner. She looked Vipulbhai right in his eyes. 'If you don't do your physiotherapy exercises or miss a single appointment, Aai and I won't talk to you forever. Talk to *him* all day then.' She nodded in Nikunj's direction.

'Ae! Why are you putting me in this? Why can't I also not talk to him?' demanded Nikunj.

'Because you will need to help him, duffer! You had one job! *One* job!'

Nikunj knew what Nikita didn't say out loud. He knew that the constipation was not physiotherapy's fault or his, but he felt too guilty to argue.

Later that night, after Vipulbhai and Ilaben went to sleep, Nikunj watched a news report on the loose motion epidemic in Kopar Khairane. The pandemic had spread to Navi Mumbai as well. The loose motion epidemic had affected the nearby SEZ areas inside Kopar Khairane's borders, and work had ground to a halt. Nikita, who was busy with her phone, suddenly looked up to see what he was watching. 'Stop watching this tatti stuff. Give me the remote.'

Nikunj, bugged with Nikita's 'one job' comment, pretended like he couldn't hear her.

She slapped his arm. 'What's your problem? Why are you sulking?'

'I have one job in the house? *One* job?'

'Shut up, ya! You know I didn't mean it like that. I was being mean to you for no reason, you know that. You do a lot these days. I'm actually quite proud of how you have become serious about taking care of Papa.'

Nikunj broke into a smile. Maybe he even blushed a little. He wasn't used to being complimented for anything he had done. Mostly because he had never gone out of his way and done anything that deserved compliments. He had lived a life only for himself and his comfort. Plus, Nikita and Nikunj didn't have a brother–sister relationship that involved communication. The only things they were used to saying to each other at that hour of the night were, 'Will you lower the volume? I have office tomorrow!' and 'You go to sleep, no? Why are you getting so bothered with the volume?' Then Nikita would give up, put on her earbuds without playing any music and go to sleep. They didn't even commit to their fights. Nikunj went to bed very satisfied with himself that night.

Nikita and Ilaben didn't speak to Vipulbhai for two days. All conversation was routed via Nikunj. On the morning of the third day, Nikita was putting on her shoes, and Ilaben and

Shardaben were chopping vegetables. Vijaybhai took a loud sip of the chai Nikunj was holding out for him, announced to everyone: 'I have forgiven all of you. I will start doing my physiotherapy exercises.'

Nikita laughed without saying anything. Shardaben shook her head with a sly smile. Ilaben gave her a sideways glance for judging her husband. (It was the ben code, like the bro code. Ben code #47: All our husbands are stupid, but we have to respect them because they are our husbands. So no ben shall laugh at another ben's husband.) Shardaben quickly straightened her face and focused on the tinda in front of her.

Nikunj patted Vipulbhai on his back. 'Thank you, Papa.' There were a couple of beats of silence as they watched Nikita make her way out the door. Then she stuck her head back through the door for a moment. 'Bye, Aai.' She paused, turned to Vipulbhai and smiled. 'Bye, Papa.'

5

Somewhere in the middle of everything, Buzzcut, Ghaps and Nikunj got their final year BA results. The three of them had scored in the forties, which meant that they had just about scraped through. That didn't matter to them though. Late that night, they celebrated with a bottle of 400-rupee sparkling wine and a few joints. They even did cheers for Raveena and Utkarsha. (Nikunj did cheers for Fehmida in secret.) Raveena and Utkarsha had both gotten distinction, while Fehmida had passed with a first class.

Buzzcut had finally stopped his bike near Raveena and had a small chat with her. They talked about how they remembered each other from class and what bench they usually sat on. Buzzcut didn't want to ask for her phone number yet. So they were still dependent on running into each other whenever Buzzcut rode past her building. Ghaps and Utkarsha had taken it to the next level and had started talking on WhatsApp.

That night, Fehmida sent Nikunj a link to her latest TikTok. The newest trend on the app was to feature four lines from the song *'Nainon mein sapna'*, and the subject of the video had to make four different changes, corresponding with each line. Fehmida had changed her outfit to match each line, as she danced to each line. Nikunj watched the video, mesmerized by the fluidity of the transitions and the grace with which Fehmida danced. They had had a few sporadic conversations on WhatsApp, and he desperately wanted to meet her, but just didn't know how to bring it up.

Meanwhile, things were quite routine at the Gholte-Butala household. Vipulbhai did his physiotherapy every morning without transforming into Madhubala. On some days, he actually became as intense as Raghubir Yadav. The afternoons and evenings were still reserved for the clinic picnic. On some days, Ilaben got more orders than she or Shardaben could get delivered on time. On those days, Nikunj would send Vipulbhai in a rickshaw, and someone from the picnic mandali would ensure that he reached there and got off just fine. Then Nikunj would deliver the tiffins and head to the clinic.

One night, Nikunj came home later than usual after meeting Ghaps and Buzzcut. Vipulbhai and Ilaben had already gone to sleep by then. Nikita was drunk again. She sat on their sofa-cum-bed with her heels still on. Nikunj could smell the Old Monk on her breath. It was the cheapest (served by the quarter) drink that all office-goers preferred when a large group went out after work. Nikita worked in Lower Parel, which had a lot of cheap bars for young office-goers. Nikita told him that some 'cool' male colleagues had treated her patronizingly, and so she'd headed out for a drink.

'Do you have a joint?' she asked him abruptly.

Nikunj jumped to his own defence. 'I'm not stoned!' The unwritten rules of the house said that everyone pretended they didn't know that Nikunj smoked. The only person to ever sneakily bring up his smoking habit was Dr Garodia. One day, the doctor placed his palm on the back of Nikunj's hand and said, 'I can fix those black lips in three sessions. I have the points to make you stop smoking also. Addiction pan toh ek bimaarij chhe.'

'I'm asking if you have a joint,' Nikita repeated.

'I don't!'

'Don't lie to me. You are stoned.'

'Okay, I'm not lying. I don't have a joint on me, but I can roll you one.'

'Good. Quickly roll, then we can go out for a walk.'

Nikunj had never expected to have this kind of relationship with Nikita. Not one to look a gift horse in the mouth, Nikunj started rolling the joint quickly. Nikita went to the bathroom, freshened up and changed into her nightie. She came out, tied her hair up and put on her slippers. 'Ready?'

The two locked the front door behind them and walked towards the nearest park. The small triangle of trees was the only green spot in the neighbourhood. The lanes surrounding the park were a couple of degrees cooler than the rest of Mulund. There was even a light breeze that night.

Nikita took the first drag of the joint, held it in and then coughed. The alcohol combined with that first hit made her body feel like jelly.

'Niku, you'll have to find a job,' she told him.

'What? But who will take care of Papa?'

'I thought you said you would figure something out.'

'Yes, I can but—'

'We've already spent more than half of our savings. Very soon, we won't be able to pay our insurance premiums. I mean, I have a company policy, but that's only Rs 5 lakh per family member. Plus, this month onwards, I will be giving Rs 5000 less towards the medical expenses.'

'Wait! What? Why?' Nikunj's pitch was one notch higher than usual. He had not expected himself to respond this robustly in favour of not making any changes to the way life was going.

'I met a boy.'

'Where? Who?'

'Will you shut up and listen?' Nikita snapped. 'He works for the client's company. His name is Abhimanyu. I've met boys before, but with this one, I want to see where it goes. So I need to pay for my share of the dates we go on.' Nikunj knew Nikita had made her life out of nothing—helping Ilaben with her tiffin business, studying hard late into the night to help land a prestigious job. And he also knew she had a life outside the family that neither Nikunj nor Aai-Papa knew much about.

'Why can't you let him pay? I mean, girls are allowed to do that, no?'

That ticked Nikita off, and she was about to turn around and snap at him but she just took a deep drag of the joint instead.

'You won't get it.'

'Why won't I? I mean, if I had a girlfriend, I'd pay for her.'

She laughed without mirth. 'With whose money?' Then she realized that she needed Nikunj in her corner. 'Okay, I'm sorry. But we're not talking about you. Is there a girl you love?'

'I don't know about love. We're just talking on WhatsApp a lot.'

'Well, I think I am in love. That's why I need to pay for my own share of the dates. I don't want to feel like I'm doing things for Abhi because he is paying for me. I want to know my true feelings for him.'

'Oh.' Nikunj didn't know what to say. Nikita had just dropped a truth bomb—one smelling of rum and pot smoke, but a truth bomb nonetheless.

'Tell me about the girl.'

Nikunj told her about Fehmida and the things they spoke about on WhatsApp. Nikita didn't say anything. She just smiled. Nikunj couldn't tell if that was her stoned smile or if she was actually pleased for him.

The two split a cigarette under the tree at the end of their lane before they headed home. Once home, Nikita applied her face pack before climbing on to her sofa-cum-bed. She tossed one of the smaller square pillows at Nikunj. 'What are you thinking?'

'I'll start thinking of what I can do to make some money.'

'Don't overreach. You're doing enough for Papa right now. Start slow. Reach a target of Rs 5000 first.' This was the first time Nikunj heard that tone of voice from her. It sounded very professional, very sane, very calculated—like she was instructing or advising a team member. Then she switched roles to being his sister again. 'Goodnight. Don't tell Aai-Papa about Abhimanyu.'

'Never! Goodnight.'

Nikita had held a secret grudge against Aai-Papa, and all the parents in the world, since her school days. A boy fell in unrequited love with Nikita in Class Ten. One day, the boy's mother discovered his unsent love notes when she was searching his bag (like all Gujarati moms do). The boy's mother went to school and raised hell. She accused Nikita of distracting the boy from his studies by fasaao-ing him in her love-jaal. Vipulbhai and Ilaben were then called to the school. They apologized and scolded Nikita publicly. Nobody wanted to listen to her side of the story. The boy just hung his head in shame, playing his mother's guilty son, grateful that his mother's wrath wasn't directed at him.

6

Nikunj did not know where to begin his job search. Ghaps asked if he wanted to sit at the shop owned by her family. If Nikunj wished to sit at shops, it would become a big hoo-ha in his family for he had refused to work at his uncle's farsan shop. 'Aavi reete beejaani dukaane thodi besaay? Friend hoy toh shu thayi gayu? Aney ee pan wine shop, maa!'

#LogKyaKahenge.

So Nikunj thanked Ghaps and told her that if nothing worked out, he would call in that favour. He also spoke to other friends who had started working as salespeople for banks. Their jobs were to stand outside ATMs, in the waiting areas of bank offices, at the banking booths in malls, and sell cards, loans and other bank schemes. They said that they would definitely be able to wrangle him an interview, but the banks always preferred people from Commerce background.

None of the available jobs called out to Nikunj. To top that, there was also the fear of failure. This was the first grown-up thing that his family expected him to do, and he had to get it right. Nikita had started helping when she was in school by assisting Ilaben with the tiffin cooking and running the house. This anxiety made Nikunj clumsy at the one job he already had. One time, he forgot to scrub Vipulbhai's back with soap. Another time, he forgot to help Vipulbhai wash his mouth after lunch. With each mistake, his self-esteem plummeted, and he started wallowing in self-pity. And when he was in the deepest trenches of this self-pity, to feel better about himself, he decided that he was the light-bearer of the household's financial responsibility. This happened when Nikunj was helping Vipulbhai bathe. He picked the one household expense he didn't like and let Vipulbhai have it.

'You know how worried Aai and Didi are about money right now? Why are you wasting money on that dhongi Dr Garodia?!' he demanded. It didn't go as he had thought it would. By challenging Dr Garodia's integrity, he had put his hand in a sleeping snake's hole. Vipulbhai lashed back in the form of a lecture about Nikunj's unemployment. Hearing his own paranoia out loud from his father only served to batter his ego further. So he left a wet and naked Vipulbhai in the bathroom and went out for a smoke. There was no one else at home that morning. Ilaben had gone to the market, and Shardaben was making the chapatis for the lunch boxes in her own kitchen that day. When Nikunj returned, he found a shrunken Vipulbhai sobbing in the bathroom.

That night, when Ilaben slapped Nikunj for doing what he did to Vipulbhai, he broke down. He did not offer any defence for his actions, and he did not stop her as she continued shouting and slapping him. Nikita jumped between Ilaben and Nikunj, sat a crying Ilaben down and asked Nikunj to get her some water. Later that night, Nikunj sat at Vipulbhai's feet and apologized for his cruelty. With some difficulty, Vipulbhai placed a dead hand on the back of his neck and shed two solitary tears, one from each eye. Nikita made tea for everyone. Shardaben WhatsApped Ilaben to ask if she was okay. Everybody on their floor had heard Ilaben scream at Nikunj. This had surprised them. Every household on the floor had had raucous fights. But no one had ever heard a raised voice come out of the Gholte-Butala household.

The next day, Nikunj was the very personification of an ideal son. He made sure Vipulbhai reached the clinic on time, right before it opened. There were a few other early birds present. Each of them was carrying a big brown bag of warm snacks in their arms like a baby. (Plastic bags had recently been banned in the city.) Dr Garodia's new assistant arrived and opened the shutter of the office. Everyone poured in. More snacks arrived. Paper plates were produced and passed around.

Dr Garodia arrived. He took one bite from everyone's plate as if to bless it and make it prasad. The younger patients were encouraged to touch his feet. Nikunj ignored the encouragement. Dr Garodia picked up a faafda from Vipulbhai's plate, put a piece of jalebi on its edge and bit the tip off. Then he placed the rest of the faafda back on Vipulbhai's plate. 'Kem, Vipulbhai? Why did you not come yesterday?' Then he picked up some papaya chutney and tossed it into the faafda–jalebi mix already churning in his mouth.

Vipulbhai lied. 'I had loose motions.' No matter how deep his faith was in Dr Garodia, he wouldn't betray his own family by telling him of the drama at home.

'See, if you don't come for one day, we go five steps behind in your treatment. Then I have to work harder. Today's session will cost you 500 rupees extra.'

'Sorry, doctor.' Vipulbhai hung his head in shame.

'Don't apologize to me. What's in it for me?' Then Dr Garodia looked at Nikunj rather accusatorily. 'Why didn't either of you call and inform the clinic?' Nikunj's guilt bounced inside him like a crazy ball shot out of a cannon. 'Next time, when anything like this happens, you should call me and tell me your father is not coming. There are a lot of treatment calculations we have to do.'

After Dr Garodia went into the AC cabin, Rameshbhai arrived with his wife and brother. Rameshbhai had fallen off a first-floor balcony and his thigh bone had all but shattered. His leg was encased in a grill designed to hold all the bone pieces in place so that they could heal. His leg also had to be kept elevated at all time, perpendicular to his body. Dr Garodia had promised that muscular puncturopathy would ensure faster regeneration of the bone. Rameshbhai hadn't missed a single session in four years.

That day, Rameshbhai and family came with faraali kachoris for everyone. Rameshbhai's face looked like a deflated balloon that day. That was weird because he was the most upbeat of all patients. He usually greeted everyone cheerfully and always had a smile on his face. His brother and his wife passed the bag of kachoris around, and then started whispering to him. Rameshbhai disrupted their whispering with a loud tantrum. 'No! I said, no! I don't want to come to the wedding. Just so that you can show off how much care you take of me. I can be on my own, you can go to the wedding!'

This was followed by pin-drop silence in the room. Everyone was used to this—patients sometimes lost their cool and lashed out at their caregivers. Rameshbhai's brother and Diksha bhabhi started murmuring to him all over again. And then once again, Rameshbhai shouted, 'Why are you forcing me? You know how much pain it will be for me to change into a sherwani?'

Vipulbhai was used to being Dr Garodia's right-hand man. This also meant that he sometimes played the role of a mediator and counsellor to families and patients. He asked Nikunj to put some faafdas, jalebis and papaya chutney on a plate and follow him.

'What's the matter, Rameshbhai? Diksha bhabhi?'

There was a wedding in the family on the coming weekend. It wasn't some distant relative or even a first cousin. It was Diksha bhabhi's youngest brother's wedding, and it was really important for everyone in the family to attend. But if Rameshbhai refused to go, then at least one other family member would have to miss the wedding to take care of him. Rameshbhai did not like hiring nurses, because he wasn't comfortable with anybody other than a family member taking care of him.

Vipulbhai resolved Rameshbhai and Diksha bhabhi's deadlock in the most Vipulbhai way possible. 'Juo, Rameshbhai, we are toh like family only, no?'

'Yes, of course, Vipulbhai.'

'Then why don't I send Nikunj to take care of you for that one day?'

Nikunj, suddenly heard his name, sat up. 'What?'

Vipulbhai continued talking for himself as well as on Nikunj's behalf. 'See, he is very good at taking care of me. I only need him every few hours. The rest of the day he's free only. So, Rameshbhai, Diksha bhabhi, what I am saying is that he can stay at your place and help Rameshbhai. Tame-tamaare jaao, enjoy the wedding full aaram se.'

All four of them looked at Nikunj, who was furious that his Papa had volunteered his services without even asking him if he was okay with it, but he did not see any harm in helping Rameshbhai out.

'Yes, I can, I mean if Papa can adjust without me for a day, sure.'

'Oh, I can adjust. I'll hold my hunger and urine, and we can plan it correctly, where you can take a rick home and help me and then go back to Rameshbhai.'

'We will be back before 10 p.m. for sure, beta.' Diksha bhabhi smiled kindly.

'And I will make sure he is bathed and ready. You only have to help him with …' Rameshbhai's brother raised his little finger. 'And if he needs anything during the day.'

'Yes, yes, he will do it. Just give him rickshaw money.' Vipulbhai placed his dead hand on Nikunj's back.

'Oh, no, no. Not just rickshaw money. It's a full-day service. We'll give Nikunj 500 rupees.'

'No, no, Rameshbhai, pagal toh nathi thai gaya? We're like family only. My son is like your younger brother.'

Nikunj too shook his head and muttered, 'You also, Rameshbhai, why are you being like this? You're like my elder brother. How can I take money from my elder brother?' Deep inside, he prayed Rameshbhai wouldn't budge and pay him.

'Think of it as your elder brother's aashirvaad, beta.' Diksha bhabhi ran her hands over Nikunj's hair and patted the back of his head.

That weekend, Nikunj earned the first Rs 500 of his life. He also learnt how to perform a catheterization. He didn't have to do it himself, but he wheeled Rameshbhai in and out of the bathroom. He was more like a catheterization assistant that day. He carried the kit and gave Rameshbhai everything he asked for—disinfectant, catheter, liquid soap. Nikunj also had to flush the toilet, because Rameshbhai's hands didn't reach the flush while still sitting in the wheelchair. In the evening, Rameshbhai had a false alarm. So Nikunj had to help him off the wheelchair, and on to the commode and back. That was the most challenging thing Nikunj had to do all day.

In their free time together, Rameshbhai told Nikunj about all the WhatsApp groups he was a part of. People with disabilities discussed their issues there and were given advice by others in the same boat. They shared life hacks, inspirational videos and songs. Rameshbhai forwarded Nikunj a video about how to help a person with disabilities access places that weren't built keeping their needs in mind. The video described how to help a quadriplegic person climb stairs, shift to a wheelchair, and so on. Rameshbhai took it upon himself to educate young Nikunj with everything he had learnt about disability from his WhatsApp groups. 'Did you know that 50–60 per cent of the people on my WhatsApp group have problems in passing motions? They have constipation. Some of them have to do DE, digital evacuation, and a lot of them take enemas.' The WhatsApp group also had disability rights activists who would invite everyone to marches and events. Rameshbhai told Nikunj about one of the events. 'I never felt like going back again. Badhaa bau bhanela-ganela loko hoy, they say everything in fast and high English. I don't understand everything they say.'

Rameshbhai called for Nikunj's help a few more times over the next couple of months. His family realized that with Nikunj's help, they could go out once in a while without having to harass Rameshbhai if he didn't want to come. It eased a lot of tension in their house, and Nikunj made Rs 4000.

Then, one day, it was Rameshbhai's turn to be constipated. Diksha bhabhi was always nervous about giving enemas, so they used to hire a qualified professional to help. Rameshbhai decided to book Nikunj for that day along with the professional. He considered the enema as a part of Nikunj's education in caregiving.

Nikunj turned out to be a natural at giving enemas. He got everything right in the first attempt. The qualified professional turned to Nikunj and said, 'Wow, tera toh bedside manners bhi mast hai. Training liya kya kidhar?'

Nikunj had learned "caregiving" from taking care of his dad. So that was the only way he knew how to take care of someone. Nikunj had to empathize with Rameshbhai the way he did with Vipulbhai to get himself to help at all. The summoning of that energy started to change something deep inside of him – much like how Peter Parker felt after being bitten by a spider – like he was changing on a molecular level.

Nikita and Ilaben allowed Nikunj to keep the money he made from Rameshbhai. Ilaben stopped giving him pocket money though. In those months, Vipulbhai's fingers too showed vast signs of improvement. He was able to hold a steel cup between the fingers of both his hands without dropping it. Of course, there was no convincing Vipulbhai that the progress was due to all the physiotherapy exercises he had been doing every morning. Vipulbhai knew, from the bottom of his heart, that all the improvement was thanks to Dr Garodia's blessings.

7

Nikita had started smiling more. At night, she wouldn't sleep till late. Instead, she would be up, texting Abhimanyu. Their client–agency relationship had moved to its next phase, towards becoming a rishtaa. The girl who kept her face carefully straight and never made a single expression after applying her face pack had now started smiling in bed. You could see the wrinkles forming on the half-dry mask in the glow of her phone.

Nikunj, meanwhile, watched a news report on the epidemic of bad farts in Borivali. Nikita was in such a good mood that the volume of the TV didn't affect her any more. She just plugged in her earphones. Romance had changed her playlist from silence to Arijit Singh and The Local Train among other artistes of Hindi love songs.

It had been a few weeks since Nikunj had met Ghaps and Buzzcut. He had started investing a lot more time in his job as a caregiver—whether it was for his father or Rameshbhai. So at night, he preferred to smoke a solo joint and then watch TV till he passed out. He hadn't even hearted the last couple of raps that Ghaps and Buzzcut had posted on Instagram. He did heart everything Fehmida sent though. But Ghaps and

Buzzcut had had enough with Nikunj's radio silence. One night, they decided to bombard him on WhatsApp with the full update of everything that was happening in their lives.

Ghaps: Utkarsha got a job at Vodafone at the mall. We meet for coffee every evening.

Nikunj: And then?

Ghaps: We just sit quietly and I get lost in her eyes.

Nikunj: 100! Osm!

Ghaps: I never remember what we're talkin about. I just remember her smile.

Ghaps: By the way, I have decided to take over our family wine shop.

Buzzcut: Ghaps ka bhajiya banne wala hai, baap aur chacha ke beech mein.

Ghaps: Roflmax. Those two idiots haven't seen each other's face since last Diwali. Apun boss hai, life full toss hai.

Buzzcut: So now no more chori from your own dukaan?

Nikunj: LOL

Ghaps: Haan, fukatchod! Chori was okay when you were getting your beer.

Buzzcut: My turn now. Raveena and I finally exchanged numbers. You know, I was all smooth like and said, 'In case, you know, I want to message you sometime.' She said, 'Sure.'

Buzzcut: 'Sure.' Those words are still ringing in my ears.

Buzzcut: So my dad's giving me the same pocket money that he did in college.

Buzzcut has sent an audio file.

Buzzcut has sent an audio file.

Buzzcut: I just got a credit card and bought all these cool apps to make beats. Check out this shit.

Nikunj: How are you going to pay the credit card bill?

Buzzcut: You know those packets of weed I've been sending you pictures of?

Buzzcut has sent a voice recording.

On the voice note, Buzzcut narrated how he started making money 'without selling out'. One day, he was chatting with their weed guy and they bonded over the rap scene. They had the same favourite artistes. 'Shake toh banta hai, bro!' the weed guy had said as they locked fists and bumped chests. Buzzcut said, 'Joint bhi banta hai, bro!' Buzzcut made him listen to his beats and some of Ghaps's raps as the two bonded some more over the joint in one of the lanes near Mulund railway station. The weed guy smiled at him and said, 'Bro, tu music banana, bro, paisa toh aa jaayega.' Then he gave Buzzcut his spare phone and explained the deal. Whenever someone called on that phone, Buzzcut had to go to their location and drop off the maal. They could negotiate the pick-up point if the buyer was willing to commute some. Buzzcut had a bike, so he had no problem doing this. The part that was the most un-Buzzcut-like about this job was that every alternate day, he had to take a train to Kasara at 6 a.m. to stock up. It was funny because Buzzcut found it impossible to wake up on time. All of SYBA and TYBA, he missed the first two lectures because classes started at 8 a.m. As soon as Buzzcut's new gig started, every alternate day, Ghaps and Nikunj received a 'good morning' message from Buzzcut along with a picture of a fresh batch of weed.

Before Nikunj could reply to the story, the WhatsApp conversation was interrupted by Fehmida's call. Nikunj picked up the phone, and she said, 'I'm sending you a new video.' And she hung up. Fehmida and Nikunj had started talking on the phone. She was allowed to visit only two places: their college and the mall. Her parents felt that college was a necessary evil, and a mall was such a public place that she couldn't be up to no good there. There was no harm in some shopping, some eating or watching a movie. (Although Fehmida didn't really shop unless there was a sale.) Much like Nikunj and Nikita, Fehmida and her brother, Furqan, also had nothing in common and barely crossed paths outside of the dining table. But unlike Nikunj and Nikita, there had been no life-changing stroke that brought them closer. Furqan was seven years older than Fehmida, which meant he belonged to the generation that wasn't interested in TikTok. Furqan was a bit more conservative in his social media behaviour. He was more of a WhatsApp forwards guy, who was a part of a dozen groups.

Fehmida got Nikunj to collaborate on some of her TikTok videos. She posted a video, and he was tasked with making reply videos featuring her video. The audio was usually a dialogue between two people. Nikunj was not the most camera-friendly person. He froze in front of the lens; his lips barely moved. After he managed to post one video, Fehmida sent him a TikTok video of her saying, 'Rehne do, tumse naa ho paayega.' Her eyes and earrings danced from side to side as she said the line. It made Nikunj laugh rather than make him feel guilty for not being good with TikTok.

That week at the clinic, Rameshbhai asked Nikunj if he wanted to take up another job with one of his friends. 'They will obviously give you money for the day's work. It's a friend from the disability WhatsApp group. His family has to be at the hospital because his younger brother's wife is pregnant.' According to Rameshbhai, the man Nikunj had to take care of was somebody genuinely fantastic.

Nikunj awkwardly asked, 'How much will they pay?' He hadn't ever imagined finding more paying caregiving jobs.

'That you talk. I haven't told them about our arrangement. We're toh like family, no?' That was code for 'feel free to ask for more than what we pay you'.

'Yes, yes, we are. I'll do it. Give them my number.'

Something about the boundary that Rameshbhai had established made Nikunj feel in control of the situation, unlike when Vipulbhai had lent his services to Rameshbhai. The line that Rameshbhai drew was also the beauty of being Gujarati. Once people establish themselves as family, they will get the most out of you, but will also ensure that you make the highest nafaas and lowest nuksaans. Gratitude is not a real thing among Gujaratis. Only elders are to be thanked verbally. Peers and juniors are to be appreciated by recommending their businesses to other people. Rameshbhai never said the words 'thank you' to Nikunj, even for basic things like passing him something he had asked for.

Rameshbhai's WhatsApp friend Kapil Karmarkar sounded and looked like a Marvel superhero. Except for the fact that he was in a wheelchair. He used to be an avid biker who lost the use of his legs in a freak accident in his early twenties. Kapil Karmarkar had maintained his upper body rigorously. He actually had four-pack abs. According to Rameshbhai, Kapil Karmarkar was blessed by the gods themselves. 'He has never gotten a UTI from regular catheterization! He just washes the catheter with tap water and reuses it. Most of us have lengthy sterilization processes.' Kapil Karmarkar was always to be addressed by his full name because of his superhero status in Nikunj's mind. According to Nikunj, nobody said Clark or Peter or Bruce or Bruce. People always said their full names. Clark Kent. Peter Parker. Bruce Banner. Bruce Wayne.

Kapil Karmarkar kept busy by helping other people with disabilities achieve their full potential. Like the man he helped by getting a specially modified car and driving lessons so that he could make money as an Uber driver. Like the girl who became a Paralympics badminton champion. Like the batch of volunteers he recruited to help a class of blind kids give their exams. He was a member of various disability communities and organizations, and participated in and helped coordinate seminars and workshops for the disabled. Kapil Karmarkar even owned a modified bike, which he used to commute around the city from his house in Thane.

For all intents and purposes, Kapil Karmarkar wasn't disabled. He was super-abled. He did almost all of his chores by himself, except for a few where he couldn't help but take assistance. One of them was the kitchen. The Karmarkar kitchen was as small as any kitchen in a suburban home in Mumbai. Only someone whose limbs functioned, and functioned well at that, could navigate this kitchen.

Another thing that Kapil Karmarkar needed help with was enemas. Kapil Karmarkar spoke in smooth, soothing tones to give Nikunj the confidence he needed to do it right. Apart from the kitchen and the enema, Kapil Karmarkar did not really need any other assistance. So Nikunj had most of the day to himself as Kapil Karmarkar shuttled around his house. Nikunj spent the day on the living room couch, and watched an entire show on Netflix. Fehmida was making him finish a Korean drama about a woman travelling back in time to stop herself from marrying the man she married. It was the most comfortable 1000 rupees Nikunj had ever made.

The only thing Nikunj did not appreciate about Kapil Karmarkar was his defence of the likes of Dr Garodia. He would say that sometimes to heal, all people needed to do was just believe in something. 'Sometimes, the body works in miraculous ways,' he said. 'If you don't believe in it, think of it as a club. The upper crust of society has club memberships, which they use for rest and rejuvenation. They meet each other, have a drink, play some cards or squash or whatever, and then go back home. Think of Dr Garodia's fees as club membership fees.' Despite Ilaben's, Nikita's and his own feelings about Dr Garodia weighing down on Nikunj, he couldn't argue the point Kapil Karmarkar had just made. 'It will take a while to let go of the hate once you start thinking differently,' he had told Nikunj.

Nikunj hadn't yet told Fehmida what he did to make money. Mostly because having two people who called him a couple of times a month did not mean it was a job. Maybe it was just a phase before Nikunj unlocked his true potential. Sometimes, he felt that caregiving would be the right career choice, despite knowing that he would never make beshumaar paisa in that career. Buzzcut and Ghaps knew about the caregiving gigs Nikunj did with Rameshbhai and Kapil Karmarkar. Utkarsha also knew because Ghaps couldn't keep a thing to herself. Raveena did not know much about Nikunj or any of Buzzcut's friends because when they hung out, Buzzcut, being Buzzcut, let her do most of the talking.

8

Somewhere in the thick of the monsoons, another of Dr Garodia's patients—Navinbhai from Ghatkopar—needed someone to babysit him for a day. Two of his family members had to go for the registration of a new flat that they had bought. Two of them wanted to go to the temple to get the blessings and prasad of some pujyashree jyotishaali maharaj who only came to give darshan once a year in the Adhik (literally meaning extra) month according to the Hindu calendar. Navinbhai had lung fibrosis, and his family was afraid that if they left him alone, he might forget to use the oxygen cylinder and stop breathing. On hearing good reviews from Rameshbhai, Navinbhai and his family approached Nikunj.

Navinbhai was a fidgety man who couldn't sit in one place for a long time. He never needed two things that were in the same room. So he was always zooming all over the house. Nikunj had to make sure that his cylinder was always next to him, and that he remembered to wear the oxygen mask and turn on the knob every time he felt breathless. That part happened quite often. When Nikunj was watching an episode of another Korean drama on Fehmida's insistence, Navinbhai gasped for air three times.

One day, Navinbhai stood at his toilet and couldn't pee. Nikunj waited outside with his phone in his hand and just one earphone in. When Navinbhai didn't come out after ten minutes, Nikunj asked if he was alright. Navinbhai was feeling blocked and it was 'burning'. That was when Nikunj remembered his school picnic to Malshej Ghat in the monsoons. The sights and the sounds of waterfalls had made him want to pee all day long. So he talked about the waterfalls and their music as the water thrashed down and the murmurs of various streams that parted ways from the waterfall till Navinbhai shouted, 'It's happening! It's happening!' Making someone pee using just his words made Nikunj feel powerful. He literally felt a surge of power leaving him and make its way to Navinbhai's body behind the bathroom door. Nikunj thought this was all in his mind, so he laughed off the thought of the 'power' he possessed.

That month, with 4000 rupees coming from Navinbhai, 1000 rupees coming from Kapil Karmarkar and 500 coming from Rameshbhai, Nikunj surpassed his monthly target of 5000. On the last day of the month, Nikita came home late. She wasn't drunk, but she was happy. She giggled and said that she had only had two glasses of expensive wine that she had paid for herself, with her own money. Abhimanyu and Nikita had gone to a fancy Italian restaurant for a date. It was an important one in their story. As she narrated the evening to

Nikunj, she asked him to roll a joint. He was excited about smoking with Nikita for two reasons. One was that he really liked that they had started to get closer since that first joint. They had actually started poking each other and teasing each other like they did in school. That was before Nikita had become a misanthrope. The other reason why Nikunj was excited to smoke with Nikita was that he was dying to tell her that he had met the monthly target that they had set for him the last time they had talked.

Nikunj and Nikita did not have a violent sibling rivalry. That was because when Nikunj was very little, Nikita had squatted on his stomach and said, 'I'm stronger, and I can kill you right now, but I love you so I won't.' That left an impression on Nikunj, and, for a long time, in his mind, she stayed as this big sister who could kill him. He just had to make sure she continued to love him. Then when Nikunj had held Nikita back from attacking that coward schoolboy's mother as Ilaben and Vipulbhai hung their heads in shame was the first time he realized that he had finally become bigger and stronger than her.

'You know, tonight Abhi and I were the versions of ourselves that we see us becoming in a few years. We see a future together.'

'That sounds beautiful, but what does that mean?'

'We went to a fancy Italian restaurant and blew most of our month's going out budget. We want to go to such places more often. Plus, last week, we went shopping and bought one fancy outfit each for this date—to represent the kind of clothes we want to wear all the time in the future.'

'Wow.'

'And you've had a good month too. You've reached your income goal! Congratulations!' She passed Nikunj the joint like she was handing him an award.

'Thank you, thank you! I'd like to thank my sister and the invention of the enema kit.' Nikunj joked to hide how loved he felt that she had been keeping an eye on him all along.

'No, but seriously. Are you happy with what you're doing?'

'I don't know. I like doing it, though.' Nikunj did not lie. Something about doing this job made him feel like he had the freedom he had always wanted, and it allowed him to take care of Vipulbhai too.

'Have you spent all the money already?'

'No, I still have 1.5 left with me.'

'Good. This time, keep the money. Next month onwards, start giving 2000 to Aai. Save 1000 somewhere. This first month is alright.'

'That will leave me with less money than my monthly pocket money in college!'

'Adults don't get pocket money, shaana!' She shook her head, 'Okay, give 1000 to Aai and save 1000. That's not too much, right?'

'I can do that.' Nikunj had thought adulting would be more straightforward, at least as simple as Nikita made it look.

'How is it going with Fehmida and you?'

'We still haven't met! We talk on the phone a lot, though. She's making me watch Korean dramas.'

'Are they like Indian soaps?'

'No, no, they are very different.'

Nikunj told Nikita all about the Korean dramas he had watched. She was really intrigued by the time travel one. The mixing of genres really warped with her head just as it had with Nikunj's. So he promptly messaged Fehmida to let her know that his sister was going to start watching Korean dramas as well. He thought that might earn him some brownie points. After Nikita went to sleep, Nikunj and Fehmida exchanged voice notes. In the last one, Fehmida asked him, 'Are we boyfriend–girlfriend now?' Nikunj didn't know what to say. They hadn't met each other since college and hadn't hung out ever, but he knew that he loved her and only her. Something about her made him happy. Every time she sent Nikunj a message (or a GIF, a link, a meme, a voice note), it made him smile. But Nikunj's inner compass refused to let him commit over WhatsApp. So he typed her a message: 'Let's meet and talk about this?'

She typed back, 'Are you breaking up with me?'

Nikunj sent her a voice note, 'No! I just want to see you face to face and say it.'

She typed, 'Then what's wrong in saying that we are boyfriend–girlfriend here on WhatsApp?'

Nikunj sent her a voice note, 'Yes, we are boyfriend–girlfriend. Happy?'

She sent him a voice note, 'Fuck you. I've already decided for both of us.'

He replied, 'What? How can you decide for the both of us?'

She ignored the question. 'See you on Sunday. At the mall.'

Fehmida was all set to meet at the mall and declare their relationship to the many shops, the food court, the multiplex and the hajaar people cruising around the gently lit and properly air-conditioned insides of the 18 lakh-square-foot box of retail glory. Except, a small bit of drama happened on Friday evening.

On Friday morning, a new challenge hit the desi TikTok scene. The audio was the '*Kannaa, panni thaan kutama varum, singam* single-*ah thaan varum*' dialogue of the movie *Sivaji*. Fehmida borrowed her brother's jacket and sunglasses to look exactly like Rajinikanth in one of the stills from the film. Raveena also participated in it, but she wasn't as committed as Fehmida. She hadn't even used a tripod or a selfie stick. Buzzcut had pleaded to both Ghaps and Nikunj to heart Raveena's video. Fehmida did not appreciate the fact that Nikunj had given the same heart to Raveena's video that he had given to hers. She sent him a TikTok–styled WhatsApp video, undubbed and in her own voice. It was the Deepika Padukone line from *Om Shanti Om*, '*Ek* TikTok heart ki keemat tum kya jaano, Nikunj babu!' She did that in full costume too—wearing a sari in the Bengali style and a big bindi.

That Sunday, before Nikunj left for the mall, he received a message from Fehmida with these instructions: 'If we bump into someone I know while we are together, we are to pretend that we are ex-classmates who just ran into each other at the mall. Post that, we will say bye to each other, go in different directions and precisely 20 minutes later, meet each other in the parking lot.'

Nikunj was thrilled because at least this meant that the plan was still on. He was finally going to meet his first real girlfriend in real life.

When they finally met in the mall's atrium, the two of them stood awkwardly facing each other. Nikunj asked her if she wanted to grab a bite. Fehmida nodded once and started walking towards the food court. Nikunj followed. He ordered a butter chicken roll, and Fehmida ordered a mutton boti roll. They ate their rolls in silence. Then they had cupcakes for dessert, also in silence. An hour into the silence, Nikunj started pleading with her every few minutes to start talking to him. He promised that he would never give a heart to anybody else. Fehmida didn't budge. She just kept checking her phone for notifications, comments to reply to and to look at the time. At exactly 8 p.m., she turned to Nikunj, put a finger on his apologizing lips to shut him up and said, 'Goodbye. I love you.' Without smiling.

9

For Nikunj, the prototype for all clients (who he had started calling patients) was Vipulbhai. The only way to help someone was the way he helped his dad—with love and respect. Getting paid for it was just a bonus he had never thought he would get for helping his dad. Helping someone like they were family came with its own pluses and minuses. The positive was that he was treated like family in return, by the patient and their kin. Whenever he needed help, they didn't behave like 'it's your job, we're paying you for it, you do it' but actually stepped up. The minus was that Nikunj gave it his all, sometimes even when the patient was a dick. And the classic example of a dick patient was Dharmeshbhai, the owner of the famous Ghatkopar House of Gathiyas.

Nikunj had met Dharmeshbhai at the clinic. Nobody there really liked Dharmeshbhai from the moment they set eyes on him. Mostly because he made a grand entry with his driver and his caregiver in a Mercedes. He always had a frown on his face. In the time that it took to transfer Dharmeshbhai from his car to the wheelchair, and the wheelchair into the clinic, he scolded his driver and his caregiver at least three times each. Dharmeshbhai had a fracture in his right leg. He was fit enough to limp from the car to the clinic with considerable ease. The thing that irked the picnic the most, according to Nikunj, was that Dharmeshbhai came with no snacks. At the very least, a Mercedes should come with a couple of packets of roasted cashew nuts.

Alpha dog points to Dr Garodia for vindicating his followers, though. He stepped out, took one look at Dharmeshbhai, and called him in. Dharmeshbhai asked his caregiver, Dhiraj, to roll him into the AC cabin. Dr Garodia showed them his hand. He asked Dhiraj to wait at the picnic with the wheelchair and asked Dharmeshbhai to limp into the cabin instead. He claimed it was his way of diagnosing the severity of Dharmesbhai's condition. Everybody at the picnic started breathing easy when they heard that. Some of them broke into smiles that translated to, 'Serves him right. Jai Dr Garodia!'

When Nikunj sneaked out for a smoke, so did Dhiraj, and that's how they became friends. Dhiraj wore pale shirts with sleeves rolled up, and the top button open. His gold chain and a smaller version of Salman Khan's *Bajrangi Bhaijaan* locket (but in gold) peeked out of his open collar as they rested on his chest. Dhiraj always wore trousers that matched with the shirt but were a shade million times darker. That day he wore dark chocolate trousers with a faintly brown shirt. On hearing that Nikunj was in the same line of business, Dhiraj opened up instantly. He had a legal property battle going on in his village in Bihar, and he needed to find a replacement for Dharmeshbhai for the days he was away. Nikunj had no patients lined up that week, so he volunteered to help Dhiraj out.

'Tereko pakka yeh karna hai Chhote?'

Nikunj nodded.

'Then tell me the history of all your patients, and all that you have done on the job.'

Nikunj rattled off everything he knew about and did with his father, Rameshbhai and the others. On learning that he had managed a wide range of situations, from an oxygen cylinder to an enema, Dhiraj was satisfied. Nikunj assured him that he was literally the unofficial caregiver for all of Dr Garodia's patients, and their relatives and friends. For some reason, this conversation made Dhiraj feel like a mentor towards Nikunj. Suddenly, he had the urge to give him advice on what would make his life better in this career. 'Chhote, you should get a bike. It will make your life very easy. And you'll save a lot of money.' Nikunj hadn't even thought about it. He was happy spending a part of his income on rickshaw rides.

One day, Dhiraj had to rush back to his village to sign some papers. He called Nikunj and booked his day, but not without a warning: 'Chhote, Dharmeshbhai is very grumpy. He hasn't pooped in three days!' Dharmeshbhai was affected by the constipation epidemic that had hit Ghatkopar. It had hit 85,000 others, give or take a few hundred, all across the area. Dharmeshbhai was worse behaved than he had ever been. Apparently, he had been throwing things at people, including food and cutlery. He had thrown a lamp at his wife. He had thrown the enema kit at Dhiraj, and screamed that he would prefer surgery to get the stools removed. It was an easy decision to make for someone who refused to get out of bed and be served all day. Thankfully, the doctors advised him to try more traditional methods first.

Dhiraj said it would be better if the two of them tried giving Dharmeshbhai an enema together first, in case Dharmeshbhai needed to be calmed down. At the very least, Nikunj would make for a good witness (one who wasn't from Dharmeshbhai's family) in case Dharmeshbhai accused Dhiraj of penetrating him forcefully with a lubed enema water tube. Dhiraj had never felt this kind of fear with any of his patients before. Nikunj asked Dhiraj why he wouldn't just let go of Dharmeshbhai. 'And what? Let someone else make this money? Chance-ich nahin!' Dhiraj was paying Nikunj from his own pocket for that evening because Dharmeshbhai's family wouldn't pay for two people: 'This is a one-man job. Why do you need an assistant?'

When Nikunj arrived at Dharmeshbhai's place, he was taken to his room by a bored-looking house help. In the room, Dharmeshbhai, who had no pants on, was waving his legs in the air (including the broken and plastered one), screaming at Dhiraj, 'If you threaten to penetrate me once more with that thing, I will call the police!' Then he looked at Nikunj and snarled, 'Don't you put a hand on me. You're just taking advantage of a handicapped man.'

'Dharmeshbhai, you really need to poop,' Dhiraj protested.

'So give me medicines. I will take as many pills, syrups and churans, but nothing is going up my butt!'

That was when Nikunj felt this urge to step forward, so he did. 'Dharmeshbhai, Dharmeshbhai, one minute, just one minute, listen to me.' His voice was as calm as Kapil Karmarkar's had been when he was guiding Nikunj. 'You want to feel better, don't you? Let us help you. I promise we will be nice and gentle.'

'Nonsense, this won't work. I won't be able to poop after this.'

'Trust me, Dharmeshbhai. Give us one chance.'

'But what if it doesn't work?' Dharmeshbhai recoiled a little. Dhiraj heaved a sigh of relief that at least he wasn't in attack mode anymore.

'I give you my personal guarantee that it will work.' Nikunj took one of Dharmeshbhai's hands in his own. 'Come on, help us help you.' Dharmeshbhai gave both his palms to Nikunj to hold. Dhiraj placed the bedpan under him. He grabbed Nikunj's hands tighter when Dhiraj slipped the lubed enema tube into him. Nikunj remembered what had happened with Navinbhai, and this was a good time to try it again. So Nikunj started talking. 'I'll tell you what will work. I want you to close your eyes and think of waterfalls. A loud, thundering waterfall, splashing its way into a valley formed by two mountains coming together.' Dharmeshbhai peed. 'Now, imagine large boulders falling down the waterfall. Big, chunky boulders. Some breaking open, some falling intact.' And Dharmeshbhai groaned loudly.

Dhiraj jumped, 'It is happening, Chhote! I haven't finished uploading the water yet.' He pulled the messy, shit-covered tube without as much as flinching. It showed how used he had become to this job when, even with poop-covered fingers, Dhiraj jumped up and down as Dharmeshbhai emptied his bowels. His face showed a drastic mood change, but it quickly returned to being grumpy as Dharmeshbhai realized he was breaking character.

On their way back, Nikunj and Dhiraj stopped for a spicy bhurji dinner. With his mouth full of pao–bhurji pulp, Dhiraj asked Nikunj, 'Chhote, tell me how you did that.'

'Did what?'

'I know you did that. I felt this connection between Dharmeshbhai and you, some kind of energy, when you were saying those words about the waterfalls.'

'Really?'

'The enema had barely begun. Chhote, I have been working since I was in college. I have grown three grey hairs and raised two kids in the time I have spent in this career. I have never seen someone who was constipated, so severely that even laxatives wouldn't work, respond so quickly to the water. It had something to do with what you said to him.'

'I really wish I knew more about this.'

'Didn't you feel any different when you were holding his hands and saying those words? Did nothing change for you?'

'I don't know, I was really focused on Dharmeshbhai …'

'Let me come back from the village. I want to test something.'

'Will you at least tell me your idea?'

'No, no ... Maybe it's just a myth. You are sure you didn't do anything to Dharmeshbhai, right? What was that thing about waterfalls that you told him?'

'That was just a thought that I've noticed helps people pee or poop.' Nikunj told Dhiraj about his Malshej Ghat experience as a child. Then he told him about how he had described the waterfalls to Navinbhai and helped him.

Dhiraj's face lit up. 'Chhote! I think my idea is correct only ... I can't wait to come back from the village. I'll take you to meet one more patient, and if you are who I think you are, Chhote, then you won't have to worry about being out of work ever again.'

The two polished off their buttery bhurji and pao, maaroed a big Thums Up dakaar and took off.

10

When Dhiraj returned a few days later, the gastric epidemic had started attacking other parts of Maharashtra. The Panchvati area of Nashik was now under the prakop of constipation along with Ghatkopar in Mumbai. The news channels had started placing a counter under their logos in their broadcasts. According to three different news channels, the numbers of constipated people in Ghatkopar and Panchvati were as follows: 1,85,438, 1,82,492 and 1,78,893.

Dhiraj asked Nikunj to meet him in one of the khau gullies in Ghatkopar. The street was crowded with three types of people—eaters, protesters and snake oil sellers. The fast food industry in the suburb was under attack from civilian associations who immediately blamed street food for the mass constipation event. The epidemic also led to a rise in alternative medicine and thus the snake oil sellers.

'Why are we eating here?'

'You don't believe it's street food that is causing the rise in constipation, surely?'

'Oh no, of course not.' Nikunj wasn't sure though.

'That's what I have brought you here to prove anyway. Come on, I want a dahi sev batata puri. What will you have?'

Nikunj picked the same thing as well. The two polished off their lunch, topping it off with lassi and a smoke. Dhiraj told Nikunj about his patient, Prafuldada, an ageing Marathi man. His wife had passed away, and his kids were in Australia. Prafuldada was clumsy and kept hurting himself. In his old age, it led to a lot of days where he needed someone to help him. One of his kids had found Dhiraj's number through some cousins and had called him from Australia to book his services. Every month, Dhiraj was sent money straight into his account. Prafuldada's life had become considerably worse since the mass constipation. He was severely affected in the fourth wave.

Dhiraj took Nikunj to Prafuldada's place, and asked him to do precisely what he did with Dharmeshbhai and Navinbhai. Nikunj found it really awkward at first. With Navinbhai and Dharmeshbhai, the feeling to help had come from within. Nikunj tried to focus but failed. Dhiraj was confused because he hadn't expected Nikunj to fail. They tried water, soap water and even glycerine, but Prafuldada just wouldn't give. When Prafuldada was too exhausted to try again, they let him rest and went for a smoke. The old man didn't complain because he had faith in Dhiraj. And Dhiraj had faith in Nikunj. Over a cigarette, Dhiraj told Nikunj that he still believed in him. Nikunj expressed his concern that they might just be torturing that old man for no reason. He finally caved when Dhiraj told him Prafuldada's life story.

This time, when Nikunj tried, he really wanted to help Prafuldada. The poor man had been lying in bed ever since his constipation had become unbearable. Dhiraj kept the bedpan in position and filled the enema bucket with water. Nikunj didn't wait for the water injection to begin, but held Prafuldada's hands and started talking about waterfalls and boulders. In no time, the bedpan was filled with gifts from Prafuldada. Dhiraj had to drop everything and lunge forward to place the urine pot right as Prafuldada squirted. When Nikunj finally looked away from Prafuldada, he saw Dhiraj smiling victoriously at him.

'Now will you tell me what all of this is about?'

'Not yet. I want to try this out a few more times. Don't complain; we're just helping people.'

Nikunj conceded that Dhiraj had a point. He promised to pay Nikunj for each session. Nikunj felt weird about taking money from Dhiraj after he had described it as 'helping people'. But Dhiraj reprimanded him. 'There's no harm in taking money from people for helping them. It's not like you're asking for diamonds or gold, Chhote! It's just 500 rupees for relief from an illness that's been bothering them for weeks.'

Dhiraj and Nikunj rode to two other patients in Ghatkopar. Both were victims of the mass constipation event. Both times, Nikunj succeeded in the first attempt itself. Dhiraj's victorious smile grew wider and wider. Nikunj was famished, so they stopped for a dabeli. They had to make do with vegetarian food because it wasn't that easy to find non-vegetarian food in the high-density Gujarati neighbourhoods. Nikunj stared at the dabeli sizzling in butter as his stomach growled. He had never felt so drained in his entire life. Dhiraj's mind was elsewhere. He was hungry as well, but his senses were numbed by happiness.

'Your smile reminds me of this girl I like. She smiles like this—full, wide, showing all her teeth,' Nikunj told him.

'She must be as happy as I am right now, Chhote.'

'Now will you tell me more about this idea of yours?'

'Yes, yes! Now that I know it's real, I don't feel like a fool talking about it.'

Halfway through their dabelis, Dhiraj said, 'Once every few decades in the medical and half-medical community, someone is blessed with the power to cure all gastric illnesses, clean the entire digestive system and make it as healthy as a twenty year old's in one poop. Doctors don't believe this. They call it an urban legend, but the half-medicals believe in it. I've never met a Tatti Raja in my life; however, the vaidyaraj who taught me everything had met the last one.'

'This is some kind of a joke, right?'

'No, I am serious. You are a Tatti Raja! You have a power, Chhote. You can make the worst constipation feel like a breeze passing through the butt; like hot knife through makkhan!'

'How does it work?' Nikunj was confused. He didn't know he had a power. But he knew he had felt something when he had helped his five patients so far. But it was just that—a feeling. 'How could a feeling be a power?'

'I told you everything I know. Maybe we can try other patients like this, and see what works and what doesn't. Maybe, if you really are the Tatti Raja of our generation, you could rid the city of this gastric epidemic.'

The transition from Nikunj just going with the flow to him putting his foot down and preparing for his destiny to unfold didn't take very long.

Dhiraj put the word out in his half-medical circles that he had discovered a Tatti Raja and was busy taking appointments on his behalf. The response blew Nikunj's mind; whereas, for Dhiraj, it only verified his belief. Everyone had at least one patient who suffered from chronic gastric problems. A lot of the patients or friends and families of the patients were also affected by the gastric epidemic. So naturally, the demand for Tatti Raja was high. People had far more faith in a stranger who came from a myth than Nikunj had expected.

If there was one value that Vipulbhai had managed to successfully instil in Nikunj, it was the classic Gandhi line, 'Vaishnav jan toh tene kahiye je peedh parayi jaane re.' Just like Vipulbhai had devoted his life to helping those who were sick in the Gholte and Butala families, and then later everyone at Dr Garodia's clinic, Nikunj threw himself into the role of Tatti Raja.

After his thirty-fifth satisfied customer, Nikunj started to feel more and more god-like. The surge of power he felt every time he made someone poop started going to his head. He asked Dhiraj if he could call himself the god of poop. Dhiraj patted his back and laughed, instead of sharing his real opinion of how conceited Nikunj had started to sound. In Nikunj's head, life had become a music video. He developed a strut in his walk and a sing-song lilt in his talk. Nikunj grew really comfortable, really fast, in the shoes of Tatti Raja. In his head, he was the star of a Telugu action flick called Tatti Raja. It had to be a Hindi-dubbed Telugu blockbuster and not a Bollywood or Hollywood big budget movie. In those, he would have had to take himself too seriously.

As time went by, Nikunj no longer needed to hold the patient's hands while treating them. He could connect his energies to theirs just by being in the same room. So he started trying different hand gestures like finger guns, fake Tai-chi moves, Hadouken among others. Nikunj even got T-shirts printed with the text 'I Do Epic Shit' in a sans serif font, which he wore like a uniform for a few days. The visual description of the waterfall and the boulders stayed the same. Sometimes, he patiently described the scenery in great detail and joy, and at other times, when he wanted to leave early, he sped through it.

Dhiraj was no less of an enabler for Nikunj's ego. He had stopped dirtying his hands with the enema tube once the boys realized that the patients no longer needed that aid. Just Nikunj's presence and words were enough. By the grace of YouTube algorithms, Dhiraj had discovered electro Latino pop music. So as soon as the patients found great relief and their eyes opened for the first time to a new world, free of their pain, Dhiraj put on a party track. The patients, any of their family members who were present, along with Dhiraj and Nikunj broke into a 30-second dance party.

Such were the heights that Nikunj's head had reached that by their fiftieth satisfied customer, he asked Dhiraj once again, 'Can I call myself the god of poop? It will have more weight than Tatti Raja.'

Dhiraj just shook his head. 'Tatti Raja is fine.'

Nikunj was shocked. Dhiraj never disagreed with him.

'I don't think we should disturb that which has been going on for ages.'

'But why?'

'My guru, the first vaidyaraj I ever worked for, used to say that is what makes the Tatti Raja even more important. He is not a god. You don't have to pray to him; you don't go to him seeking philosophical answers, or perform rituals and make bhogs in his name. There is no god of poop according to our scriptures. A Tatti Raja should do what he's best at—cure people of stomach illnesses. Do you understand how important this makes you in this time of tatti wala pralay?'

'Yes, I do. But what if there is a god of poop?'

'If there was a god of poop, Chhote …' Dhiraj paused. 'And I really believe, unlike my guruji, that there is a god of poop. And maybe the Tatti Rajas are his prophets, dishing out poop-related miracles to tell us of his existence. God knows we need some hope in these gastrologically dark times when an epidemic is playing pin-the-donkey with a map of Mumbai.'

Nikunj nodded.

'Whichever way I think about it, I know that I have to stand by you—like a younger brother, like an assistant, whatever you need,' Dhiraj continued.

While Nikunj was tripping on being the Tatti Raja, he still hadn't assimilated what it truly meant for him and his life. Dhiraj's sudden sincere confession caught Nikunj off guard. And he always felt a little weird when Dhiraj went sincere on him like that. Mostly because Dhiraj was older than him.

Nikunj hadn't yet told Ghaps and Buzzcut about him being Tatti Raja. He was afraid they would just make a joke about it. And that was precisely what happened when he finally told them after helping over eighty people. The first person he revealed himself to was Fehmida. He opened with, 'I am the god of poop.' Fehmida couldn't stop laughing. She didn't leave his side as they walked through the mall, but she didn't stop laughing. Every time she stopped laughing, she turned to look at him and started laughing again. One of the reasons that she continued laughing even after she was done was that she didn't know what to say to him. What surprised her was that despite Nikunj's ridiculous-sounding job, she wasn't embarrassed to be with him. That night, she went home and made a TikTok video using a clip from the song *'Jaane jaan dhoondhta phir raha'*. She changed locations and costume in the video. For the first *'Mujhko awaaz do chhup gaye ho sanam, tum kahaan?'*, she was in a salwar kameez in her room, and then switched to pyjamas in the loo, *'Main yahaan!'*, and repeat for the next *'Tum kahaan?'* and *'Main yahaan!'*

Nikunj felt a little upset because, thanks to the video joke that she made, he felt she didn't understand the nuances of his job. He wanted to call her and tell her, 'It's not my job to poop, it's my job to help people, to treat them. Poop is just a medium of treatment!' But he was afraid of fighting with Fehmida, worried that she might give him the silent treatment again.

After the Fehmida fiasco, Nikunj decided to tell Ghaps and Buzzcut about his powers over WhatsApp. He really had expected his friends to be more impressed by his abilities. He was used to being adored by his patients, and more so by Dhiraj. Buzzcut and Ghaps didn't reply at first. A few hours later, Buzzcut sent an audio file to their WhatsApp group. Buzzcut had made a beat out of fart and poop sounds that he found on the internet. Ghaps rapped a few lines:

'Tatti devta, tatti hi deta,

batti jalata, bedpan bajata,

paet mein galatta?

Call tatti daata!'

Then she broke into a version of *'Murgiwaalon apni murgi sambhaalo'* from Amitabh Bachchan's *Jaadugar* except she sang, 'Tattiwaalon apni tatti sambhaalo, Niku hua hai deewana.'

The track ended with a sample of a group of men laughing, with fart noises interspersed between the laughter. The problem with the song was not that it was funny, nor that it made fun of Nikunj. The real problem was that it was catchy, and it wormed itself into Nikunj's ear. Now, the track played in his head every time he entered a patient's room, like a wrestler's entry.

11

After the experience Nikunj had with his friends, he didn't want to tell his family about the latest developments at his job. They had been showing real pride in the fact that Nikunj was gainfully employed. Ilaben said to him that ever since he had started contributing to the family monthly income, the load on her shoulders had dropped a little. She had been tense for decades with the constant worry of her family's month-to-month expenditure. Now that both her kids were doing well, she didn't feel so alone in shouldering the family's responsibility. And because her shoulders relaxed, her spondylitis retreated considerably, and she stopped being in pain 24x7. 'You know, for the first time in my life, I feel like everything won't come tumbling down if I stop working,' she told Nikunj.

Of course, Vipulbhai knew about Nikunj's work because Rameshbhai and Dhiraj told him everything. One morning, he put his trembling palm on Nikunj's shoulder and said, 'Niku beta, I am really proud of you. You're doing god's work.' (Also, of course, Vipulbhai told Ilaben about Nikunj's Tatti Raja thing. Ilaben, at first, didn't believe him, but later decided that it didn't matter as long as Nikunj was happy, contributed to the family and found himself a socially productive career.)

On the days Nikunj had the time to take Vipulbhai to the clinic, his father wouldn't stop gloating to all the other members. He couldn't stop bragging about how busy Nikunj had become with helping people. 'He has an assistant also. You know that boy, Dhiraj, who sometimes comes to drop me to the clinic when Nikunj is really very busy?' Rameshbhai would also glow when Vipulbhai spoke of Nikunj. After all, he was 'like family only, no?' Plus Rameshbhai felt personally responsible for kickstarting Nikunj's career.

Dhiraj felt Nikunj was now capable of handling his Tatti Raja duties by himself, and did not need any more hand-holding or a hype man with a Bluetooth speaker. Plus, there was money to be made from the caregiving jobs too. So he told Nikunj, 'Why should opportunities go to waste when there are two of us? I'll take the caregiving jobs, you continue being the Tatti Raja.'

Nevertheless, Dhiraj continued handling the Tatti Raja appointments for Nikunj. Every morning, Dhiraj sent Nikunj names, numbers and addresses (with GPS locations) of the people he had to meet. Some of these were patients whom Nikunj had to visit. Some were local half-medical practitioners or paramedical staff who had themselves amassed a small group of patients at somebody's home, and Nikunj saw them one after the other.

Nikunj felt his power get stronger with time. With the people who weren't disabled and didn't need to sit on a bedpan, he guided them into pooping from the other side of a bathroom door. With the epidemic lashing through the city, the demand for Tatti Raja never went down. Dhiraj told Nikunj to hike his rates. So he started charging Rs 1000 per patient if it was a single patient visit and Rs 500 per patient for groups bigger than 5.

By then, Nikunj had started using the words 'treating someone' instead of 'making someone poop'. He had seen all kinds of patients and bedrooms by then. The rich had automatic beds with many buttons on them. The poor borrowed or rented cheap wrought-iron cots like the ones in hospitals in old movies, because they had no beds in their homes. They slept on the floor all their lives, and, upon getting the illness, had to find the cheapest available beds. The middle class used the beds they always used.

Dhiraj's friends in the half-medical community started exchanging stories about Nikunj. In the stories, he was often compared to a Dr Panda, who was a famous heart surgeon. The famed tale about Dr Panda was that he had teams of assistants waiting at the different hospitals he consulted with. It was the teams' job to keep the patient ready for surgery before the doctor entered the surgery room. He would enter the surgery room and start fixing the hearts like they were on an assembly line. Then the assistants would patch up the patients after he was done.

The day Nikunj made Rs 15,000, he decided it was time to tell Nikita about the changes in his life. He bought a 2000-rupee bottle of sparkling wine, rolled a joint and waited for Nikita to come home. Afraid that she might also laugh at him like Fehmida, Buzzcut and Ghaps, he smoked the joint he had rolled and then rolled another one.

When Nikita finally got home that night, she didn't sneak in like she usually did. She kicked the door open and then slammed it shut. Nikunj switched off the TV and jumped up, holding the bottle in one hand and the joint in the other. In response, Nikita angrily tossed her bag on to her sofa-cum-bed.

'Why are you so happy?' The frown on her face was hard enough to drive cracks in diamonds. Her disregard for the big green bottle and the joint killed Nikunj's drive to celebrate.

'Nothing, nothing. You tell me; what's up?'

'That bastard is showing his true colours.'

'Who? Abhimanyu?'

'Who else?' Nikita wouldn't sit down. She paced back and forth in the short passageway in the living room made by the two sofa-cum-beds. 'Bastard was all progressive till it came to the matter of surnames.'

'Wait a minute! Are you two discussing marriage?'

'No, nowhere close.' She glared at Nikunj. 'We were just having a general conversation. He expects me to take his surname! Can you believe that shit? It's 2018!'

'No, I don't!' Nikunj hadn't given that particular issue any thought because he was a guy. He saw no harm in agreeing with Nikita though. 'But don't worry; I'm sure it's just a knee-jerk opinion. I'm sure he'll change it once he has actually thought about it.'

'Sure. Else I'll fuck his happiness.' Confident of the fact that if he didn't bend to her will, she had the power to fuck his happiness, Nikita got the light in her eyes back again. 'What was your thing?'

'Oh, no, nothing.' Nikunj still hadn't caught up with her mood shift.

'Shut up and tell me before I get angry again. I can see the bottle of wine and the joint. We only drink and smoke when we have something to tell each other.' The funny thing was that she was the one who had made that rule, and this was the first time that Nikunj was using the rule for himself.

'I made Rs 15,000 today!'

'Congratulations!' She hugged him.

That gave Nikunj the courage to tell her more. 'I am also the god of poop.'

That broke the hug. Nikita moved back a pace, touched his forehead with the back of her palm. 'You have a fever? Are you alright?'

'No, seriously!'

'No, seriously, tell me! Are you experimenting with drugs other than pot?'

'No, I am serious!' Nikunj told her how he had the power to make people poop and how that was helping him treat so many people who were affected by the gastric storm that had hit Mumbai.

'Did Dr Garodia do some jaadu-tona on you? You sound like him.' Nikita couldn't stop being a woman of science.

Nikunj appealed to her rational side by telling her about the different patients he had cured with his powers. But she refused to believe it.

'Not you, Niku! I don't want to lose you just when we have started getting close to each other.'

'What do you mean lose me? I'm still here.'

'Not that way. I don't think I'll be able to respect you if you become an alternative medicine guru—'

'What? My powers are real!'

'Or you are just like Dr Garodia. You have your own community of patients and even an assistant!'

That touched a nerve and planted a seed of self-hatred inside Nikunj. He never wanted to be Dr Garodia, but looking at things through Nikita's lens, he couldn't help but see himself as another Dr Garodia, claiming his magical treatment worked.

The next day, in a fit of rage and self-doubt, Nikunj found Abhimanyu's phone number on the internet. He called Abhimanyu and introduced himself. Despite the fact that Nikita had never introduced them, Abhimanyu was more than happy to hear from Nikunj. 'Don't tell your sister you called me, okay? She'll be really upset.'

'She's already upset with you, Abhimanyu.'

'Yes, I know, but what is in a name? Your sister will be just as lovely even with my surname.'

'You better think it over once more. If she stays mad at you, you'll have to answer to me.'

'Did you call to threaten me?'

'Why don't you think about waterfalls? Huge, thunderous waterfalls, splashing down a hill—'

'I need to go … I need to pee.'

'Now, think of big boulders falling down the waterfall with the water—'

'Argh!' Abhimanyu screamed into the phone. 'I need to go; I'll call you later.'

'You see. I can make you shit your entire system out if I felt like it. Remember this the next time you make my sister angry.'

'I was going to agree with her anyways. I'm sorry, this won't happen again!'

That night, Nikita came home in a rage once again. She slammed the door shut and then leapt at Nikunj, slapping him with both her hands. She kept screaming, 'What the fuck is wrong with you?'

'You didn't believe me when I told you I am the god of poop!'

'So you torture my boyfriend to prove your powers?'

'I thought two birds, one stone.'

'Fine. You're the god of poop. I still don't believe it though; but I'll agree with you only if you promise you won't do something stupid like this ever again.'

'Okay, I won't try to help you again.'

'NO! You won't do something stupid like abusing your powers like you did today!'

'Yes, I promise.' Nikunj still didn't see what he had done wrong. He did feel some shame for making Nikita so mad. She didn't talk to him for a few weeks after that.

12

Nikunj's first Ganesh Chaturthi as a responsible adult who contributed to society was a big one for the Gholte-Butala household. All four of them bought one set of traditional wear and one set of casual wear each. This was the first time since the death of Vipulbhai's mother (Aaji) that the Gholte-Butala household hosted Ganpati at their house.

Ilaben decided to ease herself into having Ganpati over at their house again. So she started with the basic one-and-a-half-day commitment. The various Gholtes and Butalas made short visits, but nobody stayed for lunch or dinner. Ilaben wanted to have at least one proper party, so she decided to host a visarjan party. The last aarti and the walk to the pond near their house would be accompanied by a fantastic dinner.

Nikita had jumped at the opportunity and said she was bringing some friends to see the Ganpati for visarjan. She wanted to sneak in Abhimanyu with a couple of colleagues for camouflage because she preferred Vipulbhai and Ilaben meet him as a friend first. (And not immediately see him in a sehra.) Vipulbhai tried to sneak in Dr Garodia's name into the guest list. But when Ilaben and Nikita both shot him a look, he said, 'Let's keep it to family and friends only.' How about that boy ... Dhiraj? He has been so much help.' Nikunj agreed to call Dhiraj. He really wanted to call Fehmida too, but he was sure she wouldn't come. Also, he didn't want to steal Nikita's big day.

A couple of weeks before Ganeshotsav, Buzzcut befriended one of his clients, who worked at a sound studio. Via him, Buzzcut started supplying weed to more than half the studio. (The others preferred hash.) He spent all his free time at the studio—getting high, learning how to use the console and the software. The sound engineer let him play when the studio was free because he had heard Buzzcut make a beat just for fun one day and was rather impressed by it. When an ad looking for assistants showed up on the studio notice board, Buzzcut and the sound engineer cut a deal. Buzzcut would get the job as long as he made sure the supply didn't stop. Buzzcut then returned his pot phone to his dealer. They hugged and smoked a joint together to celebrate his new job. His dealer promised Buzzcut that the studio's needs were his responsibility thereon. 'Apne bro ka sapna poora ho raha hai, bro! Tu bindaas reh!'

Buzzcut and Ghaps wouldn't have made it to the Gholte-Butala Visarjan party either because Ghaps was taking Utkarsha to the Ganpati pooja at her shop. She wanted to introduce Utkarsha to her parents. Her parents were relieved to see that Ghaps finally had a close female friend. That naked heterosexual camouflage, which was entirely a creation in her family's mind, and the lack of a need to lie gave Ghaps a kick. She wanted to love fearlessly, and she was getting to. Utkarsha was more than happy to accompany Ghaps. Buzzcut was going to spend time at the studio, which was going to be empty because a lot of employees had Ganpatis at their own homes or Ganpati poojas to go to. He had taken on a lot of grunt work from the seniors. Buzzcut saw this as the only way to get familiar with all the equipment and software. The seniors had all promised him studio time in exchange for the grunt work.

It was good that neither Buzzcut nor Ghaps could make it. Nikunj was tired of them being mad at each other. Ghaps had been overly active on some anti-reservation Facebook groups. She wanted to contribute, so she used one of Buzzcut's beats to make an anti-reservation rap and posted it on the group. Buzzcut was pissed because he believed that if not for reservation, he wouldn't have been friends with either Ghaps or Nikunj. But Ghaps refused to understand that.

Ghaps wouldn't listen to anything that Buzzcut tried to tell her. She claimed to believe in the anti-reservation cause since the system was being misused and seats were going to waste. Good, deserving upper-caste candidates were not getting the opportunities they deserved. Buzzcut showed her a cartoon about racism in America. In the comic, a black boy helped a white boy get on to a platform in the first panel. In the second, when the black boy asked the white boy for a hand, the white boy refused, saying, 'I got here on my own, and you should be able to too.' When Ghaps said, 'I don't understand', to that, Buzzcut stopped arguing.

From that day, Buzzcut and Ghaps hung out with each other only when Nikunj was around. There would be no conversation. The three of them played PUBG because it did not require them to talk to each other outside of screaming directions, instructions or cuss words. With the Tatti Raja money that Nikunj had saved, he bought a second-hand iPad on OLX to play PUBG, because he didn't want to miss out on replying to Fehmida's messages as he played.

On the evening of the visarjan, everyone was in their finest kurta–pyjamas and saris. Nikita fidgeted with her phone, waiting for Abhimanyu and her two camouflage friends to arrive. Abhimanyu had shared his location on WhatsApp, so Nikita checked her phone every couple of minutes to see where he had reached. Dhiraj's two kids popped salted cashew nuts from the tray of dry fruits on the coffee table (which came out from the corner it was tucked away into only when guests arrived). Ilaben and Shardaben were busy decorating the tiny Ganpati's tinier pandal in the living room for the last time that year. All kinds of sweets and savouries were being offered as prasad to Ganpati. Dhiraj's wife was in the kitchen helping Ilaben with some last-minute frying of khoya ghugras.

Dhiraj got a call. He answered the phone and suddenly his face became serious. He said no a few times. He said, 'It is not possible. There's a big family pooja here.' He stepped out into the common area between Nikunj's house and Shardaben's house. 'It's not about the money. No, no, you are not listening.' His face showed that he seemed to be falling for the persistence he was facing. He said, 'Okay, I'll call you back.' Then he called Nikunj outside as well.

'Chhote, there's a patient ...'

'Ask them if they can wait till tomorrow.'

'No, no! It's urgent. The man hasn't pooped for many years now.'

'That is physically impossible. Are you sure that this is not a prank? Also, if they have waited for years, then they can wait until tomorrow morning.'

'But, Nikunj, understand a little. They said they would pay 10,000 rupees for the visit, Chhote.'

'It's not about the money! This is one day that Aai wants to celebrate at home. It's the first Ganesh Chaturthi we are hosting in years. Nikita's friends also haven't come yet.'

'Chhote, this doesn't sound like a prank. They said they will give you the money whether you make him poop or not.'

The 'or not' really bothered Nikunj. 'What do they mean by "or not"? I can make anyone poop.'

'They want you to go today because the mahurat is perfect. The timing has to match the visarjan hours. You'll just about make it on time to Juhu if you leave right now.'

'They should find the next mahurat then.'

'After years of looking for different ways to poop, they have developed strange superstitions and beliefs. The next good mahurat isn't for days. They just want to try you once and give up if it doesn't work. That's what they have been doing for years now—trying different things and moving on.'

When Nikunj didn't budge, Dhiraj went to Ilaben and told her about the offer. Ilaben didn't think twice before asking Nikunj to go. 'You don't get opportunities to help people on such a good day. Ganpati will understand if you choose to help a stranger, instead of staying with your family for the visarjan.'

'Think about it, Nikunj,' Dhiraj added, 'The patient is in pain with no end in sight; at least let's help them get rid of the pain of hope.'

'Fine, fine! I'll go. But I'll go alone. Dhiraj will stay here and celebrate Ganpati visarjan with all of you.' For Nikunj, this felt more like a challenge. He couldn't deal with the fact that the patient did not really have faith in his power. Nikunj was just somebody the patient wanted to try out, as if he was some snake oil seller like Dr Garodia. Whenever Nikunj compared himself to Dr Garodia, he'd get even more pissed off and try to do the most overly good thing with an extra amount of enthusiasm.

Ilaben ran her hand over the side of Nikunj's face and said, 'Vijayibhava.' Nikunj touched her feet and headed out in his fancy kurta-pyjama.

13

Kalpesh Sheth lived in a large bungalow in Juhu. Next to his house was a grand temple. It was primarily a Srinathji temple, but it had smaller areas for other gods as well. The house was a couple of streets away from the famous vada pao stall, the one where even celebrities stopped for a bite in their cool cars.

The Sheth bungalow was covered entirely in marble, from the inside and outside. The white was so pristine that there were two men whose sole job was to keep cleaning different parts of the house to ensure everything stays white and doesn't atrophy into shades of brown or green because of moss. The only two other colours on the outside were gold and green. The gold was from the flower pots, the gate, the railings and every other metallic object. The green came from the plants.

The Sheths ran a successful ayurvedic medicine business. The highest-selling flagship product of the company was Param Churna—the one-stop solution for all stomach-related illnesses. It was so big that they could afford a prime-time TV commercial. The Sheths believed in giving back to the community. Shantibhai and Vimlaben Sheth and their three sons had a considerable investment in the temple near their house and its associated charity. On that day, the entire Sheth family was at the temple for the big Ganpati pooja. Everyone except Kalpeshbhai and his wife, Kashmira bhabhi. They were waiting for their mahurat with Tatti Raja.

The house help who opened the door told Nikunj that Kalpeshbhai and Kashmira bhabhi were waiting for him in their room. The two scampered across the ominously giant house. Half the lights were switched off, and one side of the house was illuminated by the blinking Ganpati lights from the temple next door. The Sheths had hired a Nashik dhol gang to play at every pooja. The pandits sang aartis over the loudspeaker, and they kept beat with the dhols. That produced a psychedelic atmosphere in the neighbourhood. Nikunj imagined Buzzcut providing a bassline to the sounds of the aarti and Ghaps rapping to it.

Kalpeshbhai's room was as white as the rest of the house, with green art all over the walls. The window panes of the room were also made of green glass. Apparently, one of the alternative therapies that Kalpeshbhai had tried was 'green therapy'. Even the water bottle and drinking glasses were green. According to green therapy, the colour green filtered only the healing properties of light and air, and kept all the other useless and harmful stuff out.

The moment Nikunj stepped into Kalpeshbhai's room and made eye contact with him, someone blew a conch at the temple as the singers finished their most heartfelt rendition of the '*Deva O Deva*' aarti. The kids fired up anars, throwing a sharp beam of light on Kalpeshbhai's face, which looked like it had been made out of sunken rock, weathered hollow by the tides of time. The din at the temple faded to prasad-seeking chatter. Kalpeshbhai's voice boomed: 'I am the God of Poop!' Nikunj felt the capital G and the capital P in his heart as he heard the words. He had been calling himself the god of poop, but this was something else.

Nikunj had a déjà vu moment. It was as if life had rewound by a minute or so. The door to Kalpeshbhai's room was still closed. A bead of sweat rolled down Nikunj's forehead as he looked around to check where he was. He had just imagined that conversation with Kalpeshbhai. When the door opened for real, Nikunj entered Kalpeshbhai's room for the first time. Someone blew the conch, and the aarti came to an end just like it had happened in his vision. Except, this time, Kalpeshbhai and Nikunj said namaste to each other. Nikunj offered his hand to Kalpeshbhai to shake, but Kalpeshbhai made a shrugging expression with his mouth. That's when Nikunj realized that Kalpeshbhai was paralyzed from neck down.

He should've guessed this by just seeing him. Kalpeshbhai's body had deteriorated considerably. He was thin and frail. In his early fifties, he had been in this 'vegetable state' for over two decades. His muscle tissues had severely atrophied. He had to be turned every few hours, so that his bedsores wouldn't exacerbate. He had one helper and Kashmira bhabhi to take care of him all day long.

What happened to Kalpeshbhai was a medical mystery. Every expert around the world had been consulted, and nobody had heard or seen a case like this. He was healthy one minute, and the next, he couldn't move any part of his body. He felt nothing but pain all over, all day long. The battery of scans and tests that the doctors conducted yielded no results. When they ran out of hope in the medical industry, they started experimenting with the half-medical and the faith industries.

Kalpeshbhai's bowel movements stopped. No matter how much he ate. Every time he ate, the constipation became really painful, adding to the existing pain. So he had stopped eating except for a spoonful of a Gujarati-flavoured health mix a day. In a kitchen full of cooks and helpers, Kashmira bhabhi made sure she made the mix herself. It was the perfect balance of nutrients and a pinch of spirulina. Once again, the medical scans showed nothing abnormal, just an empty stomach. The doctors refused to perform exploratory surgery for no reason.

Before Nikunj could introduce himself to Kalpeshbhai, Kashmira bhabhi stormed out of the bathroom. She wiped her hands on a napkin hanging on the plastic hoop by the door while asking Kalpeshbhai, 'Is the Tatti Raja here yet?' Then, on seeing Nikunj, she turned to him and did a namaste. 'Oh, you must be Nikunj Gholte-Butala?'

'Yes, I am the Tatti Raja.' Nikunj returned the namaste.

'Yes, we know.' Kashmira bhabhi spoke as though she and Kalpeshbhai had already known the secret that was just revealed to them.

'I didn't think it was a secret …' Nikunj lied.

'It may not be a secret, but it was an urban legend until you showed up.' Kalpeshbhai smiled. 'Nobody had seen or heard of a Tatti Raja for decades now.'

'We know because we've been looking,' Kashmira bhabhi added.

'We have been through too many dhongis claiming to be the next Tatti Raja till we heard some of your miracle stories. We have actually given up. We're just going through the motions.'

'Haha, nice one.' Kashmira bhabhi laughed at Kalpeshbhai's 'motions' joke. 'So don't worry, you won't disappoint us if you fail. Please come in and work with us with no pretence. Let's see if your powers are for real.'

Mr and Mrs Sheth's jaded levity and flippant disbelief poked Nikunj's already raging ego. Despite having the half-medical industry as a part of his daily life, Nikunj refused to see the apathy it inspired when it failed an ailing person consistently for decades.

'Oh, I will show you how real my powers are.'

Kashmira bhabhi and Kalpeshbhai just smiled. Someone blew the conch at the temple once again. The Nashik dhol gang began playing again. Nikunj assumed some kind of a Kung Fu stance as if to intimidate the Sheths (who stayed unfazed). He really wanted them to feel the power. He moved his hands around like he was summoning some kind of energy from the universe. Then he Hadoukened his hands in the direction of Kalpeshbhai's stomach and said to him, 'Close your eyes, and imagine a waterfall. Tall, loud, thunderous, splashing and smashing through rocks to form a puddle over decades.'

'Aaahh!' Kalpeshbhai's right eye twitched, and he had a moment of relief.

'He just passed urine. He's wearing a diaper so you can't see,' said Kashmir bhabhi.

Kalpeshbhai laughed. 'Come on! You're the Tatti Raja! You can do better than that. I don't have peeing problems. Anybody can make me pee. She helps me with a catheter thrice a day.'

Nikunj whipped his hands through the air a few more times, assuming different, fake, Kung Fu stances, before Hadoukening in Kalpeshbhai's stomach's direction once again. 'Now, imagine giant boulders dropping down the waterfalls with the water. Big ones. Causing great splashes in the pool below.' Nikunj's pitch had gone up, and he started to sound more desperate than fearsome.

Kalpeshbhai laughed louder and louder. His eyes rolled back, and his head pushed back against the pillow. Tears rolled down the side of his eyes. Nikunj continued describing the giant boulders falling. Kalpeshbhai's laughter escalated until it sounded like a broken scream. Kashmira bhabhi jumped at Nikunj. 'Stop it! He's in so much pain! Don't cause him more pain!'

Kalpeshbhai was out of breath. He laughed gently through his tears. 'You were making poop run down my system with your powers. But it refused to come out.'

'That just causes him more pain.' Kashmira bhabhi was by Kalpeshbhai's side, gently stroking his forehead.

Nikunj woke up to his surroundings in a flash, and he had tears rolling down his cheeks. He had just tortured an already unwell man only to prove his powers. He had done the exact opposite of what he started out doing. He just wanted to help people—not to torture them or impress them with his powers, like Dr Garodia. As long as he helped people, it shouldn't have mattered if people believed in his abilities or not.

'I'm sorry! I am so sorry!' He ran to the side of Kalpeshbhai's fancy automatic bed.

'It's okay. At least we know that you are a real Tatti Raja.'

'I don't know why that didn't work. It always does; even on a phone call!'

Nikunj pulled himself together and sat on a chair. Kashmira bhabhi offered him a glass of water, which he finished in silence. Every now and then, he glanced at the flickering lights from the temple.

'Kalpeshbhai, I'd like to try my best to help you poop,' he announced.

'I'd like that, Nikunj.' Kalpeshbhai smiled warmly for the first time since Nikunj had entered their room. There was no longer a challenge in his tone or expression.

'I'm going to cancel all my morning appointments and spend every morning with you. We have to figure out a solution.'

'By the way, why did you do those Kung Fu moves when using your powers? From the stories we have heard, the Tatti Raja doesn't need to do any of that to summon his powers.'

'I don't know. I just felt I needed to impress you, win your faith with some intimidating dramatics.'

The helper knocked on the door. 'It's time for the pooja.'

Nikunj stepped forward and insisted on helping shift Kalpeshbhai to his wheelchair. He was glad for all the training that Rameshbhai and Kapil Karmarkar had given him. Kashmira bhabhi helped Nikunj put on the straps that held Kalpeshbhai in place. After the pooja, Kashmira bhabhi insisted on getting a dabba of prasad packed for Nikunj's family. Before he left, Kalpeshbhai and Kashmira bhabhi fixed a monthly retainer of Rs 1 lakh for Nikunj to work with them.

14

By the time Nikunj got home, the visarjan party was over. Nikita, Abhimanyu and the two camouflage friends were hanging out outside the gate of the building, passing two cigarettes between them. Many windows and balconies in the neighbourhood bragged about hosting Ganpati with colourful, blinking lights.

Nikita waved Nikunj over from across the street. As he crossed to get to them, she could see the dejection on his face and the disappointment that weighed his shoulders down.

'Hey, you! What happened?'

'I'll tell you later. I'm just going to freshen up.' Nikunj opened the dabba of prasad from the Sheths. 'Here's some prasad.'

'I borrowed some fuljaris from some friends. Come back, and we can light them up over a smoke.' Nikita was clearly hinting that she needed to give Nikunj the full download of all that had happened at the visarjan party.

'It was really nice to meet you guys,' Nikunj said as everyone took a piece of prasad from him. 'I rarely get to meet Didi's friends, but I need to go freshen up now. See you soon.'

It had been a big day for Nikita. She had never really had any close friends since the incident with the boy in school. Her then best friends had sneaked to the back of the crowd when the accusing finger was pointed at her. Since that day, she had only been driven to make a great life for herself. Like she had to prove to everyone at school or just to that boy's mom that she would never be with a boy who had such a low intellectual level. Once in a while, she would check on everyone at school on Facebook to see how well she was doing compared to them. Her independence was obviously one of the primary parameters of her comparison. Else, she wouldn't have been able to compete with the more affluent kids or the ones who married rich boys.

By the time Nikunj changed out of his sweat-drenched clothes, took a shower and changed into his night shorts (the ones with a hole in them) and a T-shirt (the one with two holes in them), Nikita had bid farewell to her friends and was back inside. When Nikunj exited the bathroom, she stood between the TV and him with a bottle of wine and a joint. She had asked Abhimanyu to roll a joint for her before he left. She was so excited that she hadn't even changed into her nightie.

Nikita's excitement dimmed upon seeing Nikunj's sullen face. 'What is wrong with you? Here I am waiting to celebrate the day, and you look like you saw a chudail or something.'

'Forget about mine. You tell me your good news first.'

'No, I don't want a bummer for later. You finish yours, and then we can open the bottle of wine for the good parts.'

Nikunj told Nikita everything that happened at Kalpeshbhai's house. Nikita, of course, did not want to believe any of this magical realism that was indirectly a part of her life too now. So she listened to everything like she would have if Nikunj had approached her with a work problem.

'This is the first time you're facing a real difficulty, young brother of mine.'

'Okay, so forget about me. I'll figure out a way around it. Else I'll have to accept that there's a limit to my powers.'

'Yeah.' Nikita didn't have any other gyaan to impart.

'You tell me, how was it with Abhimanyu and Aai–Papa?'

She blushed, picked up the bottle of wine and unscrewed it. 'I can't even tell you! It was amazing! Aai was so impressed with Abhimanyu. That's why I had gotten those two for contrast. I had told them just to be guests. So when Abhimanyu got up to help Aai in the kitchen, she was toh fully glowing. Later she asked, who is this boy? He's so well brought up.'

Nikita and Nikunj went to the building terrace with the joint, wine bottle and the fuljaris. They sat on the tank and watched the Ganpati processions go by on the street below. She told him about Abhimanyu and her plan to arrange for a similar 'friends' meeting with his parents. Then, on Valentine's Day, they planned to seek parental blessings for their coupledom. 'Based on today, I am sure Aai will give us her blessings.'

It had been a big day for Vipulbhai as well. As much as he liked to believe otherwise, the months of physiotherapy had started to show results. His hands were healing. At the visarjan party, Vipulbhai showed off his newly acquired finger strength by serving modaks to everyone with his own hands. It took a while and a lot of concentration for each one, but everybody cheered him on heartily. According to Nikita, the living room had turned into a stadium, and Vipulbhai was a batsman who was hitting six after six with each modak. 'Come on, uncle! You can do it! Ho jaayega! Yes, yes! Good grip! Not too hard or the modak will crumble!' Nikunj wanted to kick himself for missing all this action.

The next morning, Nikunj woke up a little dehydrated and with a small hangover. The house was flooded with the aroma of navratna korma. Ilaben and Shardaben were busy cooking up a frenzy to deliver a 'comeback' after the day they had taken off for the visarjan. Nikita had already snuck the empty bottle of wine out with her when she had left for work. Nikunj regained full consciousness while he helped Vipulbhai finish his morning routine. He obsessed over one question as he got ready and ate Aai's upma for breakfast: What was he going to do to help Kalpeshbhai? This was the first time he was as lost as he was when college had ended. Except, he wasn't worried about money this time around. He was going to be more than well compensated.

The Sheth household was buzzing when he got there. Some of them were getting ready to head to work. Some of them were already working. Some were sitting at the dining table and eating breakfast. Each family member had one servant following them, helping them go through their day at 100 per cent efficiency. The kids were still sleepy and had slathered themselves on the couch next to their grandfather (Shantibhai aka Mr Sheth Senior), watching a news report on TV about the gastric storm. The epidemic had reared its ugly head in Indore, Madhya Pradesh. Nipania in Indore was under a diarrhoea attack. Compared to the ominously silent house from Nikunj's last visit, this looked like an entirely different place.

Kashmira bhabhi was eating upma for breakfast. Kalpeshbhai sat in his wheelchair at the head of the table. Kashmira bhabhi would give him one spoon of upma at some point because that was all he could have without inviting the pain of constipation. 'Come on over,' he called out, spotting Nikunj. 'What will you have for breakfast?'

'Nothing, I already had upma for breakfast.'

Nikunj and Kalpeshbhai waited for Kashmira bhabhi to finish eating. Her daily routine centred entirely around Kalpeshbhai. Every morning, she would wake up an hour before Kalpeshbhai. In that hour, she would finish her workout, take a shower, reply to the good morning messages on WhatsApp in the family groups, and then send wishes to family members and friends who had their birthdays, anniversaries, etc., on that day. Then she would go to the in-house temple, and offer prayers on behalf of Kalpeshbhai and herself. Kalpeshbhai had stopped believing in god, and he only went to the temple with the rest of the family so as not to give them a shock by publicly denouncing religion.

Since Nikunj was going to handle Kalpeshbhai that morning, she had her first time out in a little over two decades. Nikunj first tried giving Kalpeshbhai an enema, hoping that if the Tatti Raja gave him an enema, it would work. Of course, the attempt failed. The soap water injected into Kalpeshbhai's butt came out smelling as floral as the soap. But through the morning, the two of them got to know each other better. Nikunj told him about how his life worked. Kalpeshbhai talked about his experiences with babas who had claimed to be able to heal him completely, or at least solve his excretory problem.

15

Over the next few days, the time Nikunj spent with Kalpeshbhai kept increasing. He would get there in time for breakfast and then hang out with Kalpeshbhai till lunch. On one of those days, Kalpeshbhai told him about how his body sometimes became a biogas plant. That's why his diet was so controlled. Not that he could eat much. It was like his body consumed every last molecule of nutrients from all the food that had accumulated, and formed a high-gravity black hole in his intestine. A black hole that misbehaved as soon as you sent more food its way. Kalpeshbhai giggled as he told Nikunj that half a boiled egg would give him a flammable burp. Nikunj laughed, 'Just because you've got this unsolved puzzle of an illness doesn't mean everything you say is true.'

The next morning when Nikunj reached the Sheth dining table, Kalpeshbhai waited with an egg on his plate. Almost every Sheth family member's clockwork-like rhythm broke that morning. They stopped on their way in, smelling the egg. Outraged, they would locate the source of the smell, and, on finding that it was Kalpeshbhai, they would just sigh and give up: 'It must be some new therapy he is trying.'

Kalpeshbhai looked down at the egg and then up at Nikunj, and said, 'Challenge accepted.'

Kashmira bhabhi cut the egg into two halves and fed Kalpeshbhai one half. Kalpeshbhai patiently chewed and swallowed the half egg and then asked Nikunj, 'Do you have a lighter?'

'Yes.'

'Then, to the shayankaksh!' he shouted joyously. If his arms had been working, he would have raised a fist in the air for sure. On reaching the bedroom, Kalpeshbhai shouted, 'Quick! Quick! There's a burp coming; bring your lighter to my mouth.'

Nikunj sparked the lighter and held the small flame in front of Kalpeshbhai's mouth. When Kalpeshbhai burped, the lighter flame turned into a little mushroom cloud. Nikunj jumped back in shock. 'Whoa!'

'I think I have a couple of more burps left in my stomach. They're taking a while to come out.'

'Wait, wait! I want to try something.' Nikunj placed the lighter in front of Kalpeshbhai's mouth, looked into his eyes and said, 'Kalpeshbhai, think of a can of Thums Up opening. Think of a half-filled PET bottle of Thums Up being unscrewed. Think of that pop and fizz sound. Think of that release of gases.'

And there it was—one more mushroom cloud exploding upwards from the lighter. This one was bigger and survived until it floated as high as Nikunj's face.

'One more! One more!' Kashmira bhabhi applauded.

'No, no! Let's keep some gas in there. If you're okay with it, Kalpeshbhai, I want to try something during the enema. I'm sure we can make you fart fire.'

Kashmira bhabhi couldn't stop laughing. She stayed in the room that day through the enema. At the end of the failed attempt to make him poop, Kalpeshbhai asked, like an eager child, 'Shall we fart fire now?'

With his legs still propped up for the enema, Nikunj took the lighter to Kalpeshbhai's colon and said, 'Think of a balloon. Think about a small hole in the balloon. Think of the balloon deflating as a small whistling current of air is released from that hole.'

A small whisper was heard blowing out of his butt as it turned into a small flame shooting outwards from the lighter. It looked like someone had installed a tiny jetpack or a small flame thrower up his butt. Kashmira bhabhi's face had gone pink with laughter. She slipped off the couch and fell to the floor. 'Saambhlo … ' she stopped gasping for air as she laughed. 'I should … hahaha … have … hahaha … pulled out my phone … hahaha … camera to show it to you!'

Even if he couldn't see the whistle of a flame shooting out of his ass, Kalpeshbhai giggled with Nikunj and Kashmira bhabhi. When Nikunj put Kalpeshbhai's legs down again, Kalpeshbhai told him, 'I like doing this fire thing only because it makes her laugh so much. Thanks for helping me make her laugh more than she has in a long time."

The disappointment of failing to make Kalpeshbhai poop at the end of every session weighed on Nikunj's soul. He carried that weight to his evening patients in whatever suburb was deeply affected by the gastric storm. But this day was different. Nikunj was happy that at least he was leaving the Sheth household with Kalpeshbhai and Kashmira bhabhi in a good mood.

On his way to Malad, he checked his phone to see Fehmida's latest TikTok video. It was the #FilterSnapCry challenge. She did three filter changes and two location changes, crying at the second location change. Nikunj grinned at how cute she looked when she fake cried. She drew tears flowing down her cheeks with eyeliner. Although, without a doubt, the real stars of that particular TikTok trend were male TikTokers. The women were good, but just the sight of men crying was making women faint with joy everywhere. The men cried through their videos, through all the filter changes and location snaps. All the songs they chose were sad heartbreak songs in Hindi, Tamil, Telugu and Bhojpuri.

Nikunj hearted Fehmida's video and video-called her. As they spoke, she asked if he could postpone his appointments and take her to Juhu beach—through the call. Nikunj and Fehmida had wanted to go to Juhu beach forever. For Fehmida, the beach was a family thing, a place to go on Ramzan nights.

'I never feel what they show in TV and movies when I see the beach. I want to feel that gudgudi wali feeling when I think of the beach.'

'Gudgudi wali feeling?'

'Don't think so much, just take me to the beach on your phone.'

Fehmida made herself a bowl of microwave popcorn and propped the phone up on her bed as she lay down and watched Nikunj at the beach. They took a long walk together from one end of the beach to the other. After the walk, she watched him eat cheese sev puri and a gola.

Fehmida tried to explain to Nikunj how he had made the beach a mast place for her—far more than it had ever been. He didn't get it. So she threw some popcorn at her phone, which Nikunj pretended to dodge at his end. 'Go now; go to Malad and make people poop!' The two laughed and hung up.

16

Ilaben and Shardaben's new thing was trying international cuisines. It all started with Toral bhabhi, who lived in 403, two floors above Shardaben and the Gholte-Butalas. Ever since she had returned from her US holiday, she was infatuated with pasta, falafel and hummus, and Mexican food (which, according to her, was closest to Punjabi cuisine). Toral bhabhi learnt how to make these dishes from YouTube videos. She would go out and buy the ingredients, even if she had to go to the supermarket in Kurla to get the right ones. Every time she experimented, she brought some to Ilaben and Shardaben to taste. Ilaben's first reaction was: 'This tastes so different, so much livelier and fresher than the pasta at the live pasta counter at weddings.'

It didn't take a lot of convincing from Toral bhabhi for Ilaben and Shardaben to join her in her experiments. Soon, the three of them hatched a scheme to start an evening kitchen. They announced the evening kitchen on Dussehra by changing the lunch meal to Italian—spaghetti and paneer balls. In the beginning, the international evening kitchen was open for delivery only on weekends. They started with themed weekends like a Mediterranean weekend (Lebanese and Greek) and European weekend (French Saturday with paneer in wine-free wine sauce, and a British Sunday with batter-fried paneer and potato chips). Toral bhabhi invested in the business by buying an oven, which they placed in Ilaben's kitchen, since that was the base of operations. The weekend evening kitchen menu was sent to all the regular tiffin customers through WhatsApp, and the team would take the fastest fifty orders. They decided to keep a ceiling of fifty orders for the trial run.

By then, Vipulbhai had fully recovered. Except for his eyes. His pupils had a delayed reaction to bright light. The doctors advised him to continue wearing sunglasses through the day and rest his eyes as much as possible. During his last trip to his doctor (not Dr Garodia), the doctor had told Vipulbhai that his reflexes had returned to those within normal range considering his age. His medication was also reduced. Vipulbhai was also complimented on the sincerity with which he followed his physiotherapy exercises. However, he still did not acknowledge that physiotherapy had helped. He was still holding on to the narrative that he did physiotherapy to keep Ilaben, Nikita and Nikunj happy. In his head, it was Dr Garodia who had cured him, and till Dr Garodia didn't give him the green light, he was going to keep getting treatment from him. In reality, he just wanted to keep going to the clinic because out there, he was someone important. In a way, Vipulbhai had returned to his original job as Dr Garodia's assistant, except he was no longer being paid. In fact, Dr Garodia took money from him for his 'treatments'.

It had been a great couple of months for Dr Garodia as well. He had moved his clinic from the real-estate office to the outhouse of a lush bungalow in Juhu, not too far away from the Sheths. Somebody finally fell head over heels for his story that he was an avatar of Vishnu. Damuben Patel, the eighty-four-year-old mother of Mansukh Patel (a prominent builder), was too afraid to get arthritis surgery, so she believed every word Dr Garodia said—mostly because he told her that he could reverse her arthritis. Dr Garodia told her, 'Arthritis is about rebuilding the bone from calcium in the bloodstream. It will take a long time and many treatments a day.' Damuben Patel was the Kokilaben of the Patel household, and thus, the mother of two enterprising crorepatis. So, in all her magnanimity, she offered the bungalow's outhouse to Dr Garodia. Mansukhbhai, who had a net worth of at least a few hundred crores, didn't bother to find out what was happening in the outhouse. He trusted his mother's decision. After all, if not for her cunning and support, his father wouldn't have been able to build the construction empire that he and his brother had inherited.

The waiting area picnics suddenly got a lot more luxurious. The picnic now sprawled across an entire household, and Dr Garodia used the master bedroom as his consultation room. But he had his own sorrows about moving to the Patel house. Because of the size of the outhouse, the waiting area didn't look as densely populated as the waiting area of the real-estate office. The true mark of a good doctor, according to Dr Garodia, was the population density in the waiting area. A few days into nursing this sorrow, Dr Garodia asked all his patients to earn good karma by bringing in their friends and family. 'Even if they have a cold. If they are healthy, I will make them healthier.' And just like that, the entire outhouse was suddenly full of waiting patients. New members joined the picnic. Dr Garodia's treatment durations dropped to half their original times.

Damuben didn't join the waiting area picnics like the other patients. She received five treatments a day from Dr Garodia. She stayed in her room the entire day—only coming out when it was time for her treatment sessions. But she made sure that the outhouse had a constant supply of tea and homemade snacks from the Patel kitchen. Suddenly, the waiting area picnics stopped being potpourris with limited food supplies, and became well-catered, all-you-can-eat affairs.

In those weeks, Dr Garodia had become bolder than a god. He had started distributing secret guru mantras to all his patients to chant while they thought of him. That would help them self-heal apparently. Each mantra was unique to each patient. Vipulbhai wouldn't tell anyone what his guru mantra was, not even Ilaben. Dr Garodia had also started asking all his patients to bring him small gifts as chadhava. These were things like Bluetooth earphones, a roti maker or a set of mugs. He only asked this of the richer bhakts. The middle-class and lower-middle-class bhakts were asked to bring smaller things, like a particular mithai from a particular sweet shop, a bouquet of flowers or sometimes just a portrait of Vishnu. He even made a small shrine in the living room of the outhouse by sticking all the Vishnu portraits on one of the walls.

Meanwhile, Kalpeshbhai had arranged for a car to pick up Nikunj in the mornings. The car would then drop him to wherever he was going in the afternoon. Since Vipulbhai also had to go to Juhu now, Nikunj started dropping him off at the Patel house. Every time the car passed farsan shops, Vipulbhai sighed loudly and said that he deeply missed taking faafda-jalebi for everyone at the clinic. He initially thought he was going crazy—he should be happy because they got fantastic food every day and Dr Garodia's practice was running so successfully from the 'new clinic'. He only felt better after he heard Rameshbhai's family discussing the same sadness. As a method of protest against the tyranny of the Patel kitchen, Rameshbhai and Vipulbhai conspired to bring their own snacks. Alas, this didn't last long because Ilaben shut it down. It wasn't just for monetary reasons. Toral bhabhi had introduced Shardaben and Ilaben to a healthy eating WhatsApp group for people in their fifties. However, Rameshbhai and Diksha bhabhi ensured that Vipulbhai met his daily farsan requirement.

17

It was Navaratri. The October heat wave had passed. The Mumbai weather was just going to keep getting better all the way till February. The humidity, the sweat, the wet mess of the rains were all on their way out. Pandals were erected inside building compounds and small durga temples inside the pandals. They hired sound systems, since hiring an orchestra band would be too expensive. The orchestra bands with singers (who participated in but did not win any reality TV shows) always performed at the big playgrounds in every area. Every night, people (mostly Gujarati) dressed in kediyas and chaniya cholis, and took to the streets to either visit each other's building sound system garbas or the big orchestra ones. From 8-ish in the evening to midnight, the streets seemed filled with loud and colourful crowds. They were either heading to a garba or returning from a garba, or taking a snack-and-soda break at one of the many food outlets in khau galli.

Buzzcut messaged Nikunj. 'Bro, Raveena and I couldn't have found a better time to take it to the next level.' The two had started going out on dates. They spent hours at cafes and the mall. Raveena dragged Buzzcut to a pre-Navaratri dandiya night, where they danced for a couple of hours before sneaking away to the parking lot and stealing a kiss. They had kissed only that one time. When Buzzcut tried again, Raveena had said, 'Maybe later.' Buzzcut had to wait a long time before Raveena wanted to kiss him again.

Nikunj barely had any time to hang out with Buzzcut and Ghaps. Those two were still not hanging out with each other. The anti-reservation fight hadn't resolved itself yet because Ghaps just wouldn't yield. All she really had to do was pick up the phone, call Buzzcut and just listen to what he had to say, but she refused to do it. She argued that she could still be right. Nikunj had had enough of the fight. He was tired of not using their WhatsApp group and talking to both of them individually. He had to type things twice. Also, he really needed to take off his Tatti Raja suit for a bit. Poop was all he thought about all day. It swirled in his head like a batch of unflushables stuck in the swirl of the flush. So he sent a message on their WhatsApp group asking both of them to be free on Sunday night to play PUBG in the park.

That evening, Nikunj decided that they wouldn't sit in the corner of the park under the tree. Since they were going to be there at night after the gate was locked, they had the park to themselves and could sit anywhere they wanted. So he decided they would sit inside the dome-shaped jungle gym, in a circle, so that they faced each other. Ghaps arrived with three bottles of wine instead of their usual beer.

She told Nikunj that her thoughts had changed since she started drinking wine. Her sadness felt more mature and grown up, and not a thing to cry to someone about. The funnier development in Ghaps's life was that she no longer needed to steal from the shop. She had been running it since her father and his brother had had another loud and pointless fight. Obviously, Ghaps said all this before Buzzcut arrived.

Once Buzzcut arrived, Ghaps focused on her phone and her bottle of wine. Buzzcut's latest inscription on the buzzed sides of his head was two hearts each. Nikunj laughed a little. 'Why two hearts, bro? That's a little thanda, right?' Buzzcut just said, 'If a hip-hop producer walks down the street with two hearts on his head, showing off his love, people know he's not afraid of anything. I'm not afraid to look uncool because love is badass, bro.'

Nikunj wasn't drinking or getting stoned that day because he had to keep his system clean for a new treatment idea that he was trying with Kalpeshbhai and Kashmira bhabhi. (We'll come to that in a bit.) Buzzcut and Ghaps must have been a bottle-and-a-half down and on their fourth game when Ghaps suddenly broke down a little. Nikunj looked up, 'What happened?'

'I think I'm a kulfi rapper. I rap about gangster friends and guns and big dick type things, but I am not like that. That is not me. That's just a fake image I'm trying to sell using my talent.'

Buzzcut snickered and then pretended like he was laughing at some player that he had just killed in the game. 'Mar, chodu!' he added for effect. Nikunj shot him a look. Buzzcut didn't look up from his phone.

'No, Ghaps, you're not.' Nikunj had to say something encouraging. He didn't understand the scene or know what was supposed to be good rap or shitty rap. They were all just rappers to him. However, he had always liked the tracks that Ghaps and Buzzcut created when they made music together.

Ghaps ranted for a while as she killed everyone in her path in the game. Her game was so strong that Buzzcut and Nikunj almost died while just watching her slay half an army of people coming at them. When that game ended, she looked up at Buzzcut and said, 'I'm sorry.'

Buzzcut smiled, his eyes red and tiny from all the wine and pot. 'You're not a kulfi rapper. You're just a rapper. But you shouldn't worry about that. Just focus on yourself, and write something honest.'

'Yeah, why don't you take the performance pressure off and just write for a while? Forget about open mics and Instagram,' Nikunj added.

The two of them ignored Nikunj entirely. Mostly because they knew while he meant well, he just didn't know anything about music.

'I can't do live and spontaneous things like diss rapping. I can think and write and come up with lines, but they all sound like somebody else has thought of them.'

'That's because you're not trying to do you. You're trying to do someone else. And you've stopped having fun doing other people.'

'I don't think I can do it. Rapping was fun in college, but maybe I am one of those people who needs to grow up.'

'Fuck diss rap. It's just grown-ass men writing poems about each other. You have a voice, Ghaps. Use your lyrics to talk like you talk to us. Tell us who you are.' Buzzcut picked the loudest garba beat that was audible in the park and played it with his finger rings on the bottle of wine. 'Come on, give me some bars. Tell us who you are.'

'I'm Ghaps, I'm sitting in a jungle gym,
With my two homies...'

Buzzcut stopped. 'You don't use the word homies when talking to us. Talk to *us*, Ghaps.'

'This is M-C-Ghaps, reporting live from the jungle gym,
The name is Gayatri, washing my sins with a bar of Vim
Sitting with two chutiyas, aur yeh Buzzcut ki hai beat
And Nikunj mein hain taaqatein to make the world sheet
Phaehle hain iss park mein, getting stoned, getting drunk,
This is we, this is hum, fuck being raja, fuck being runk
Facebook se bani chutiya, phir gaali khaai sab ki
Yaaron ke dil todke, yaadein bhulaadi love ki
Jab aankh khuli toh saans phuli toh maa chudi toh gudgudi
Jo dost dukhi toh jag dukhi toh wine bani Chandramukhi
Subah ki thhi bhooli ab shaam ko main laut aayi
Darkness ko chhodke main bulb waali thought laayi.'

This made Buzzcut smile. Having pleased him, Ghaps felt free to let loose a little. The next couple of verses had a lot more levity to them.

'This is MC Ghapaghap reporting from the after dark
I'm the mother of rhymes, tere dragons ki maa ki aankh
Sitting with two chutiyas, I got Buzzcut on the beat
Sadda Nikunj has the powers to make the world sheet
Pee rahein iss park mein, with some ganja and PUBG
This is we, this is hum, bas yaaron mein rab ji
Mutton se koi beef nahin but fuck roti sabji

And fuck champagne, usse bhara hai bathtub ji
Mere chat mein koi sticker nahin cause I'm a text-whore
Dekh chhote teri wicket giri, cause you're a big bore
Liquor ki koi fikar nahin cause I always have more
Hide all your girlfriends cause I own the "lick her" store.'

Both Buzzcut and Nikunj cheered as she wrapped it up with a slowdown on the last line. Ghaps just blushed, leaned back against one of the rods of the jungle gym and took a long sip from her bottle of wine. Buzzcut raised the bottle he was playing on. 'See, I told you!'

Over three more games of PUBG, Buzzcut and Ghaps updated each other on their lives while spewing gaalis at other players and sometimes each other. The three of them finished all the wine and weed they had come with.

Later that week, Ghaps started spending more evenings in the small office at the alcohol warehouse behind her shop. She called Buzzcut over, and they turned it into a small studio for themselves. Ghaps told Nikunj, without telling Buzzcut, that Utkarsha had started getting a little jealous of the time that Ghaps was spending with Buzzcut. She didn't tell Buzzcut this because he had always been paranoid about Utkarsha being their Yoko.

18

From Ganpati to Dussehra, Nikunj, Kalpeshbhai and Kashmira bhabhi tried everything. There were no bad ideas. Kashmira bhabhi had the bright idea that if Kalpeshbhai felt weightlessness, his bowels might loosen up. So the three flew to New Zealand to jump off a plane and have Nikunj use his Tatti Raja powers as they felt the weightlessness of falling forever.

It did not work.

On landing, they double-checked Kalpeshbhai's diaper just in case he didn't feel himself poop because of the weightlessness. He just felt pain. Kashmira bhabhi had a blast though.

The next thing on the weightlessness list was scuba diving. Kashmira bhabhi found the closest scuba diving destination (perfect for that time of the year) in Indonesia. They ordered special oxygen helmets for Kalpeshbhai and Nikunj, so that they could communicate with each other using earpieces. Suspended in the middle of the ocean, when Nikunj tried his powers on Kalpeshbhai, they failed to yield any positive results. Once again, they double-checked the diaper inside his scuba suit. Nothing.

Kashmira bhabhi had been sending pictures of these trips to the family WhatsApp groups, and everyone was cheering for Kalpeshbhai. His father, Shantibhai, used a mobile app to Photoshop images of gods giving their blessings into the pictures Kashmira bhabhi sent and re-uploaded them to the WhatsApp group with words like, 'Bless you, son and daughter-in-law!' and 'May God add your joy, subtract your illness, divide your pain and multiply your wealth!'

Finally, when they couldn't trick the body into feeling weightless, they decided to go for the real thing. Kalpeshbhai called one of his cousins, who called one of his cousins who worked as an engineer at NASA. The plan was to try the same flight that Stephen Hawking had achieved zero gravity in. It was the same plane that NASA astronauts used to train for their space flights, called the Vomit Comet. A few days before Navaratri, they blasted off on a parabolic path in the air to give them a couple of hours of gravity-free time. Once again, Nikunj's powers did not work on Kalpeshbhai.

After the failure of the weightlessness experiments, the three of them decided to take a break and go back to the drawing board. Kashmira bhabhi took the morning off, and went to the salon and spa near their house. She felt guilty leaving him alone, but Kalpeshbhai insisted that even he needed a morning away from her and Nikunj (to stew in self-hate).

On the third morning of Navaratri, when Nikunj reached the Sheth bungalow, Kalpeshbhai and Kashmira bhabhi were not at the dining table. One of the servants told Nikunj that the couple had not left their room since the morning. By then, Nikunj had presumed that he was a part of the team. So he entered the room without knocking. That's when he realized that no matter how much he did to help them, he would never be a part of their team in this fight. There were parts of the sickness that he wasn't even ready to face. There was no way he would understand or accept them. The scene at play when Nikunj entered the room was one of those.

Kashmira bhabhi was straddling Kalpeshbhai's stomach as he lay on his bed. Kalpeshbhai was naked. There were a sponge and a tub lying next to the bed. She banged her open palms on either side of Kalpeshbhai's forehead over and over again, like how Jerry slammed cymbals on either side of Tom's face in *Tom & Jerry*. Kalpeshbhai grunted and screamed words between the head claps, 'Why. Is. This. Happening. To. Me?' He gritted his teeth in agony. The agony was not from being struck in the face over and over again. That was just a distraction from a more substantial pain that was consuming him.

Nikunj should've apologized and walked out of their room till they were ready for him. But all he could do was jump forward and grab her hands. 'What are you doing? Stop!'

Kalpeshbhai screamed, 'Why did you stop?'

Both Kashmira bhabhi and Kalpeshbhai noticed Nikunj at the same time. Nikunj let Kashmira bhabhi's hands go, and she hopped off the bed. 'We're sorry you had to see this!' she gasped, as Kalpeshbhai rushed to explain, 'I was just having one of those frustrating mornings where I can't see any good in my life and the world. Because I can't throw a tantrum by slapping my own forehead, she was helping me with that.'

Nikunj was really shaken. His eyes welled up. He wanted to tell them, 'You don't have to justify anything to me. I'm here to help you.' But all he said was, 'Whatever you say.'

Nikunj had only ever seen Vipulbhai hurt himself like that in the middle of an argument with Ilaben. He would slap his forehead a couple of times, but then realize it was futile to hurt himself. That display of anger against the self to get the attention of the other was nowhere as horrific as what he saw Kalpeshbhai doing. Kalpeshbhai's anger against himself came from self-hate. For him, there was nobody really left to blame for not having shown up to help him. There was obviously no god. There was nothing left to have faith in. Kashmira bhabhi felt a mixture of shame and guilt for helping her husband exercise his self-loathing.

'I'm sorry, I'll just step out for a bit if you guys want to freshen up a little.' Nikunj's bedside manners kicked in as they fought their way out of a brain–body deadlock.

'There's no need for that, Nikunj. I should get dressed. Why don't you help out?'

As Nikunj helped Kalpeshbhai with his track pants, the couple told him that the cause for that morning's hopelessness was a bedsore that wouldn't give up. The bedsore that looked like the map of Maharashtra had won some real estate since Nikunj had last seen it. The pain and the bleeding had been making him twitch and spasm. The collagen padding had stopped helping any more. (They had tried everything from antibiotics to aloe vera and the only thing that had healed the wound was collagen.)

At night, Kalpeshbhai had spasmed himself to the edge of his bed, and his body pushed itself against the protective railing. Kashmira bhabhi had taken a sleeping pill, so he didn't want to wake her up by shouting loudly. Then she wouldn't be able to fall asleep again and would have a terrible day. He spent the night awake, spasming, with nothing to think of but his inability to even roll over.

Kalpeshbhai was finally ready, so Nikunj buzzed the bed upright. Then he helped strap Kalpeshbhai's upper body to the bed so that they could sit face to face. Kashmira bhabhi stepped out and arranged for breakfast to be sent to the room. Over breakfast, the three of them decided to try a more conservative approach to solving their problem. Kalpeshbhai and Kashmira bhabhi told Nikunj everything that they had tried over the last twenty years. Maybe the answer lay somewhere in there. Perhaps they needed to revisit something that sounded like it would work but with the Tatti Raja's powers. A lot of crazy stories came out of this exercise.

The most villainous thing they had done was spiking half a suburb's (Goregaon East) milk supply with a chemical that constipated people. It was their crazy, rebellious younger days. They thought that causing a stress point in the poop-time continuum may attract the Tatti Raja. A week into that, Kalpeshbhai's brother, in an attempt to open their eyes, took them to visit Goregaon East. They realized what they had done immediately. People were irritable and violent. Many hadn't slept properly in days because they couldn't.

Kalpeshbhai and Kashmira bhabhi realized that they had made the classic supervillain move of inflicting their pain on to the world. That was the last time they tried something that crazy. 'It was a wake-up call,' said Kashmira bhabhi. 'We were out of control. We started therapy after that.' Nikunj asked if they had anything to do with the gastric epidemic that was terrorizing Mumbai and now finding its way to other parts of the country. They said they were shocked by what was happening, and, of course, they had nothing to do with it.

19

Finally, Kalpeshbhai and Kashmira bhabhi remembered one therapy they had tried but had forgotten about. Mostly because it was a forgettable experience—for it was literally a dream. They had tried lucid dreaming, where a lucid dreaming expert, Kashmira bhabhi and Kalpeshbhai would go under and meet each other in the dream world. The expert and Kashmira bhabhi would try and plant suggestions in Kalpeshbhai's mind to make him poop. In the dream world, Kalpeshbhai always worked hard to focus and managed to find himself a toilet. But as soon as he sat on the toilet, the dream would kick him out and he would wake up. Nikunj didn't know if any of that was even possible. But he really wanted to know what lucid dreaming felt like, so he agreed to try Tatti Raja powers on Kalpeshbhai in the dream world.

When Kalpeshbhai suggested this, he said, 'We'll have to meet each other in the dream world. Do you have any experience with this?'

'I have no idea what you are talking about,' said Nikunj, 'but I am open to trying things. If I can make people poop with just my words, then what's to say what's real and what's not?'

'Great! While trying lucid dreaming therapy with me, Kashmira did a basic course as well. There are a few rules to doing this.'

He turned to Kashmira bhabhi, who chimed in, 'Keep your body clean for a few days. Cleanse it of alcohol, tobacco and drugs. The cleaner you get the more strongly we'll be able to connect on the dream plane.'

'That can be done.' It was easier said than done for Nikunj. He was too exhausted at the end of the day after treating groups of patients in Ulhasnagar.

'Let's try and eat at least a couple of meals together in the day, so that our body chemicals are synchronized perfectly.'

'I can have breakfast and lunch with you.'

'Don't work out or stress yourself physically in any way. Try and increase ghee in your diet.'

Kalpeshbhai, Kashmira bhabhi and Nikunj set off on a new mission, Mission Inception. They had as many meals together as possible. Sometimes, when Nikunj would leave in the afternoon, Kashmira bhabhi packed him dinner. (Of course, Kalpeshbhai only ate a spoonful at all the meals, but still.)

Every night, after the Navaratri noise died down, Nikunj messaged Kalpeshbhai and Kashmira bhabhi to let them know he was going to sleep. In the build-up to Dussehra, Kalpeshbhai and Kashmira bhabhi started appearing in Nikunj's dreams. Or, as they called it, 'We are having shared dreams. Now, to put it to work.' On the first night, they just ran into each other on a street above which snakes flew like birds, but without wings. When the dream changed, they vanished. The next morning, Kalpeshbhai told Nikunj that he needed to concentrate, direct his mind towards Kalpeshbhai, and make an attempt to stay in the dream longer. 'One of the ways to do this is to focus on your hands in the dream. As soon as you realize you're in a dream, look at your hands and keep staring till you feel you have control over yourself.'

On the fifth night, Nikunj had a dream where something or someone in a forest was chasing him. He couldn't recall what it was when he woke up, but on his run, he remembered Kalpeshbhai's advice. He stopped running and looked at his hands. Suddenly, Nikunj achieved a conscious state in the dream. He started thinking about finding Kalpeshbhai and Kashmira bhabhi. That's when a cottage appeared in the middle of the forest he was in. In the cottage, he saw Kashmira bhabhi, Kalpeshbhai and three cups of tea laid out. Kashmira bhabhi sat on a broken chair, and Kalpeshbhai paced back and forth, swinging his arms in a circle like he was warming up in the stands before going out to bat. Kalpeshbhai overused his arms and legs in the dream because here was the only place where he could be his complete, total, healthy self. Nikunj lasted in the shared dream until he finished his tea. Then he was thrown into the middle of the forest once again.

Two nights after Dussehra, Nikunj achieved full control over his dream state. As Navaratri progressed, he learnt some new things. One was that if he held Kalpeshbhai or Kashmira bhabhi's hands, he was able to stay in the dream longer. So that night, he held Kalpeshbhai's hands in the dream and finally used his powers. 'Okay, look into my eyes. I want you to imagine a waterfall. A huge one. Bigger than and taller than the Niagara Falls. Thousands of tonnes of water thrashing down on the rocks, making this loud noise. Now, imagine giant boulders, as big as small hills, falling down the waterfall.'

Suddenly, the reality of the dream started to fall apart. At first, the cottage tore itself apart like an invisible storm had struck it. The three of them found themselves in the middle of the forest. Kalpeshbhai and Nikunj didn't break eye contact as Nikunj continued to describe the waterfall, and boulder after boulder crashing down. It soon turned dark in the woods, lightning bolts flashed, and the sound of thunder caused more ruptures in the dream. The forest tore itself apart from around them, and all three of them were left in nothing but darkness. Kalpeshbhai finally closed his eyes and vanished. Kashmira bhabhi disappeared right after him. Nikunj also woke up.

He looked around to check where he was. He heard Nikita snoring, the fan chopping through the air, a distant rickshaw kick-starting, and a faint Arijit Singh and his guitar pouring out of Nikita's earphones. He picked up his phone and saw it was 4.38 a.m. The phone buzzed in his hand. Kashmira bhabhi had sent a photo of a golden turd in a diaper. The turd had a faint phosphorescent glow around it.

'Is that gold?' he wrote back.

'Yes.'

'Wow. Please give my congratulations to Kalpeshbhai! Shall I come over right now?'

'No, we'll sleep now. You should also get some real sleep.'

Nikunj put his phone away and tried falling asleep. But he couldn't, so he stepped out for a smoke. While smoking, he messaged Fehmida to see if she was up. She was. She was preparing for the #LickAStatue challenge on TikTok. She felt too shy to actually go in public and try that. Plus, she only went to the mall, where there were no statues. There were mannequins, but she felt that licking a mannequin would be a little creepy. And yes, obviously, she was also afraid of even trying to lick a statue in public. In India, it was dangerous to act lewd with a statue. Mostly because all the statues were those of eminent personalities (whom a lot of violent people were deeply and emotionally invested in). She video called Nikunj to show him a balloon. She was pasting paper with a mixture of glue and water all over it. She planned on making her own papier mâché statue, even if it was just the face.

Tossing and turning, Nikunj waited till he heard the first rustle inside the house. It came from Ilaben waking up to collect the delivery of milk, curd and paneer for the kitchen. He jumped out of bed and helped her carry the dairy products into the kitchen, and then he hit the shower. This was the first time in Nikunj's life that he was the first person to bathe and get ready in the house. That day, he didn't wait for Kalpeshbhai's car to pick him up. He dropped a message to Kashmira bhabhi and booked an Ola.

It was a long ride from Mulund to Juhu. Nikunj found it much longer, despite the roads being relatively deserted that early in the morning. He fidgeted with his phone all the way to the Sheth bungalow. He ran straight to Kalpeshbhai's room as soon as he reached. None of the family members or servants even blinked as he passed them. They had gotten used to having him around.

Kalpeshbhai was propped up with a small table placed in front of him with some breakfast on it. He looked really disinterested in the poha. Kashmira bhabhi sat next to him with a spoon in her hand, but made no effort to feed him. Despite the fan chopping through the air above them, the room was absolutely still. Everything smelled stale from their sadness.

'What happened? Why aren't you guys happy? Kalpeshbhai finally took a shit.'

'So what? Nothing changed,' said Kalpeshbhai glumly, as Kashmira bhabhi added, 'There has been no improvement in Kalpesh's condition.'

'I'm still in just as much pain as I was yesterday.'

'All we have is one golden turd. We could've bought it and kept it in the bedpan to make ourselves happy.'

'Did you buy that golden turd?' asked Nikunj. He knew that if anybody could afford that much gold, it was Kalpeshbhai.

'No, not at all!' said Kashmira bhabhi at once. 'The miracle of the golden turd was fascinating till it waned and we realized that nothing else has changed. Kalpesh can't even move a finger.'

'We can't give up so quickly. Let's see if he poops tomorrow. We'll try this again tonight when we sleep. The change has just begun.' Nikunj was entirely winging it with his confidence and hope now. Somewhere, in their heart of hearts, Kalpeshbhai and Kashmira bhabhi knew that this was it. They had waited for this day for so long that they hadn't considered the idea that maybe nothing would change even after he pooped. In their heads, they had attached his healing to his ability to poop.

The three of them met in the dream world every night. Every night, Nikunj tried his powers, but they didn't work. Then he had the bright idea of administering laxatives in the dream world to see if they could trick his body. It didn't work. Once again, everything was back to square one. Kalpeshbhai's piles acted out again. The Maharashtra-shaped bedsore decided to buy more property on Kalpeshbhai's butt, causing more pain and spasms. The three of them were back where they began, not knowing which way to head, or what to try next.

20

In the week after Dussehra, Abhimanyu found the perfect excuse to introduce Nikita to his parents. It was his birthday, and he wanted to host a party. He invited the two colleagues whom they had used as camouflage at Nikita's place and two of his best friends from school, whom he was still friendly with. They met once or twice a week and hung out. Nikita had already met them a few times as well. Abhimanyu thought it would be a good idea to invite Nikunj too. After all, he had to have a good relationship with Nikunj so that a misunderstanding like that surname shit wouldn't happen again. Nikunj had powers; so he couldn't be messed with. Also in consideration was the fact that Nikita loved Nikunj to bits. Nikita, of course, categorically told Nikunj to make an excuse and decline the invitation.

On the night of Abhimanyu's birthday, Nikita got home a little past 1 a.m. That morning, Abhimanyu had just bought a car on EMI, so he dropped her home after they took a long drive in it. He had packed some birthday cake for Nikunj.

Abhimanyu felt like the day had gone in his favour and decided to push his luck. He told Nikita that he was going with her to the house. He wanted to say hi to Nikunj, and give him the cake and a joint in person. Nikita was highly amused by the effort Abhimanyu was putting in, so she just shrugged.

When they entered, Nikunj made his 'extra load of patients' excuse in person.

'That's alright,' said Abhimanyu. 'You're out there helping people.'

Nikunj opened the Tupperware container of cake and went to town on it. Abhimanyu waited awkwardly as Nikunj stuffed himself. He hoped that the brother–sister duo would light the joint with him. Nikita decided to leave him hanging awkwardly and did not help at all. A few minutes of silence later, Nikita said she needed to sleep and sent him off.

As soon as Nikita shut the door behind him, she jumped to the window. She waited for his car to leave. Then she jumped back to Nikunj with a wide grin that she had been suppressing ever since she left Abhimanyu's house.

'That sneaky bastard! I told him how you and I have bonding conversations on big nights, and he was trying to sneak into the one tonight.'

'Why would he do that? And we're having one tonight?'

'I guess he wanted to know how it went with his parents. And yes! I just met his parents!' Nikita was going to tell Abhimanyu everything after she made him wait a little. When people said, 'Information is power', she really believed in it.

'So, how did it go?' Nikunj's mouth was still gooey from the last bite of cake.

'Not like this. We have to do it right. Let's go down and smoke this joint.'

She didn't bother to change into more comfortable clothes and take off her heavy earrings; she was bursting to tell Nikunj everything. The brother–sister duo went down and started their walk around the neighbourhood. They lit the joint at the first turn. Nikita was really proud of the classic courtship move that she had pulled on Parul aunty, Abhimanyu's mother. She had Facebook-stalked Parul aunty and memorized everything she found. Nikita had also learnt that Parul aunty was a self-proclaimed gourmet chef, so she had asked Toral bhabhi for her YouTube playlist of international cooking videos.

Abhimanyu told Nikita that his mother was making Italian for his birthday. So Nikita went to Nature's Basket and bought a block of parmesan cheese to take along. Of course, Parul aunty and Nikita got along like a house on fire soon after aunty saw the pack of cheese. It blew her mind. As she grated it over the pasta in the small Borosil tub, she smiled to herself like she was giving her blessings to Nikita, and said, 'Finally, at least one of Abhimanyu's friends understands good food.' Nikunj high-fived Nikita at the end of this story. Nikita, who wasn't really a high-five kinda person, accepted it graciously because that day had really been high-five-worthy.

The only part of the plan that somewhat backfired was Abhimanyu's dad. He told Parul aunty that Nikita talked too much. In reality, he felt suspicious of how quickly aunty had taken to Nikita. Parul aunty asked him to shut up and go to sleep. 'What do you know about women?' she said sagely, before turning around.

21

In one of her solo trips to the mall on a weekday, Fehmida discovered an abandoned corridor. The next time she visited with Nikunj, they managed to sneak in two chairs into that corridor. That was the first time they chilled there, away from the eyes of all the other visitors and security cameras. Over the next few trips, they snuck in empty boxes (to make a table out of), trays, tissues and condiments. On another trip, the two of them went shopping. They bought a tablecloth for their little box table, eight colourful tea candle holders and a pack of tea candles. Then they bought two floor cushions because sitting on the chairs wasn't the most comfortable, especially if they wanted to lean against each other.

Fehmida and Nikunj started meeting on Sunday evenings as well. Obviously, they never left the mall. Once, they had sneaked off to Juhu beach, but Fehmida didn't want to do it again, because while it was exciting, it came with a lot of anxiety. The mall became a small world they owned. And now, they had a small house in this little world. It was their Eden, and no snake could get them to bite the apple that brought them back to the reality of the world outside. They spent hours there, sometimes without even talking to each other.

She would reply to her fan mail and comments, or watch TikTok filmmaking tutorials on YouTube. Nikunj consumed all the content served to him on WhatsApp—forwarded jokes, videos, songs, inspirational stories and sometimes even educational stuff from the disability group that Rameshbhai and Kapil Karmarkar had insisted he join. Sometimes, Fehmida and Nikunj just leaned against each other at a corner table of the food court and watched whatever Korean drama Fehmida had gotten both of them hooked on to.

For a few weeks, Fehmida had been rather quiet. Something had been eating her on the inside. All her replies had become curt and monosyllabic, even in text. Nikunj assumed that it was something he did. He asked her what was wrong. He asked her if she was mad at him about something. She video called to tell him that she wasn't mad at him at all. Then she showed him the papier mâché statue she had been working on for the (well, passé) #LickAStatue challenge. Not being able to participate in it was driving her over the edge. She said she wanted to make a #LickAStatue video even if it was after the trend died. Nikunj offered to find her a gargoyle or something at VT station to lick, and they could go there at night when there were very few people around. He needed a distraction from his search for the meaning of the golden turd. Fehmida refused the gargoyle offer and said she'd figure something out.

Then one mid-November night, she sent Nikunj a lot of dancing emojis on WhatsApp. She asked him to meet her at the mall. By that time, the mall was mostly shut, except for the multiplex. Even the food court outlets had closed their counters, and were cleaning up and locking down. Fehmida arrived with a big bag and a giant roll of paper. The two of them sneaked away to their secluded, abandoned corridor.

Fehmida rearranged the chairs to face each other. She sat Nikunj down on one of them. She then unrolled the poster, which was a high-resolution printout of a picture of a garden. That was going to be the frame for her video. She moved his chair to ensure that he was right in the middle of the frame.

'What are you doing? Can you tell me? I can maybe help you if I knew what we're doing.'

She pulled out the items from her bag. 'Will you just shut up for once? Why don't you think some more about Kalpeshbhai and the golden turd?'

'Is that why you're upset with me? I'm thinking too much about work? I'm so sorry; I didn't mean to ignore you.'

'No, no, I'm not being passive-aggressive. I really need you to not care today. You're not my boyfriend today, you're a prop.' That was the first time either of them had dropped a label for their relationship face to face. Nikunj felt that he needed to respond before it was too late.

'Oh … Okay … Are you sure you're not mad at me for something, girlfriend?'

'No, no …' She laughed at his failed attempt at being smooth. 'If I were mad at you, I wouldn't be talking to you at all. Don't you remember?'

'Yes, I do.' Reassured that she wasn't mad at him and that she had called him her boyfriend, Nikunj resumed thinking about the golden turd, what it meant, and how to make it happen again.

Fehmida opened two bottles of colour—one black and one white. She mixed the two on a small plate to make a stone grey. She then poured water into two plastic cups and dipped two brushes in one of them—one wide brush and one really thin. 'Okay, now don't move too much. Try not to smile or move your eyebrows, or make any expression with your face.'

'Why? What is that?'

'It's food colour; chill! Now stop moving your mouth.'

Over the next half hour, she slowly painted his entire face grey. She kept blowing on the thick layers of paint to make them dry faster. '*If* you make any expression, the paint will crack, and you won't look like a real stone statue.'

Nikunj knew he didn't have any choice but to comply; however, he'd have liked it if she had at least pretended to ask him before using his face as a prop. With her face so close to his, he could feel her warm breath when she wasn't blowing on the paint to dry it. He so badly wanted to kiss her. Their physical relationship had never crossed certain lines. The fourth time they were at the mall together, the two started holding hands when they walked. In the weeks closer to Diwali, on never being caught by any of her family or neighbours, they started walking with their hands wrapped around each other's waists. Ever since they found that secluded spot, they started giving each other long hugs, which went on for several long and deep breaths.

Once Fehmida was done painting Nikunj's face, she pulled out thick soap water from her bag, mixed some glue with it and started working on his hair. She combed it stiff and blow-dried it with her hair dryer, which she plugged into the one working socket in their corridor. 'Don't touch your hair. It will wash away, don't worry. I tested it on my own hair first.' Then she painted his hair as well. When she was done and happy with her work, she took a picture and showed it to Nikunj. Her contouring work was entirely on point. Nikunj looked like he was made of real stone, except for his eyes. She asked him to close his eyes and went to work on them. She pasted his eyelids shut with surgical tape and painted over them. She contoured two stone irises on the eyelids. 'Now, don't move your eyeballs under your closed lids. And control your breathing.

'Okay, we're ready ... I'm going to set up my tripod and then lick you.'

Nikunj wanted to open his eyes and say, 'WHAT?!' But he was trapped. He couldn't, not without pissing her off at least.

Fehmida returned to his side and said, 'Five, four, three, two, one ...' She went quiet and then Nikunj heard the song she had chosen for the challenge. It went, '*All these people drinking lover's spit ...*' Fehmida's wet, warm tongue slowly licked the food paint off the side of Nikunj's face. He tried his best to not move, to not smile, even when the wetness tickled. In a few seconds, the song loop ended, but Fehmida didn't stop. She lifted a leg, wrapped it across his lap and clung to his side. She clutched his face with both her hands and went to town on one side—like his face was an ice cream cone.

Nikunj took that as a hint and moved his face sideways to kiss her. She backed off immediately. 'I told you, don't move.'

'Okay, okay … I won't. Can we get back to what we were doing?' Nikunj pleaded without opening his eyes.

'No, now the paint has cracked on one side. We're done.'

'Did you at least get your shot?'

She didn't say anything. She just got off Nikunj's lap and jumped to the tripod to check the video she had made. Then she showed it to Nikunj. With the garden poster in the back, it really looked like Nikunj was a statue in a park that Fehmida had licked. Then she applied the slow-motion filter to it to tie the video to the mood and the tempo of the song, and uploaded it to TikTok.

By the time Nikunj and Fehmida reached home, the video had 566 hearts. The next week, her work made it to at least four different #LickAStatue compilation videos. One of those video makers had actually edited her footage into his original compilation and re-uploaded it to YouTube. The TikTok post, as well as the YouTube videos, got a lot of chamdi comments. Fehmida had warned Nikunj of her fan base and how she interacted with them. She had been flirting with a couple of guys on TikTok, but it was just friendly flirting, 'without crossing any lines' she had said. She told Nikunj that she had very strictly warned them: 'No meeting, no WhatsApp, no hanky-panky messages. I will block you if any of this happens.' She also had a couple of women TikTokers as friends. They often made reply videos to each other's work.

To top this core group of fans who got attention from Fehmida, there was also this small group of ardent male followers. They had made a Facebook group called 'TikTok Beauty Queen Fehmida's Male Slaves'. They would photoshop their bhakti-ras all over screenshots taken from her TikToks or selfies from her Instagram. They claimed to be waiting for her to command them to do things. Some of them messaged her and asked her to send them her 'feet water' (water collected from washing her feet). All this male attention did make Nikunj a little insecure. Not that he had any reason to worry. He told himself that he found it amusing that so many men were so disconnected from reality. They had no idea what Fehmida was really like. They just worshipped her online image. He found strength in the fact that he was the only person she was on WhatsApp with.

Not that Nikunj's insecurity had escaped Fehmida's notice. She always knew when he sulked silently as she read out the comments she got. In fact, sometimes she'd read out the pervy ones just to annoy him a little. Only so that he would hug her tighter whenever they hugged next. One night, she felt like going on a proper date with Nikunj. So she gave him a list of items to buy from the food court and meet her at their spot. When he returned with the packed food, she had switched off all the lights in the corridor and set up a candle-lit dinner. She'd placed the chairs on either side of their little box table. Fehmida played French acoustic indie pop on the Bluetooth speaker to make it seem like a high-class candle-lit dinner. The two of them arranged the plastic cutlery in the manner of high-end restaurants. That evening, they felt like their mall corridor had been transported to a whole other plane. Both Fehmida and Nikunj felt slow and feverish as they ate with closed mouths and smiled at each other, celebrating the perfect moment that they had made for themselves. The only thing that didn't happen that evening was a kiss. And Nikunj was really dying to know what Fehmida would taste like. The smell of her perfume gave him a light buzz every time he was around her, and if she touched him even once, he broke into a smile. After the many days and hours that they had spent together, being around Fehmida really overwhelmed his entire body.

22

The winter chill that vacationed in Mumbai for a couple of weeks every year had just landed. It was a week before Christmas. These were everybody's favourite holidays—one week placed right between the Diwali holidays and the summer vacation. Ghaps had gone underground to deal with her existential sadness and her kulfiness as a rapper. The only person she spoke to at length was Buzzcut when they hung out at the studio. She tried to write something real, something that she truly felt. She even replied to Utkarsha's messages with one-word replies. None of this helped Utkarsha's insecurities. Utkarsha tried to understand Ghaps's pain and was being damn civil about the way Ghaps had disconnected. But every now and then, Utkarsha would snap and send a passive-aggressive message. However, the passive-aggression in her texts was lost on Ghaps.

A couple of days before Christmas, Ghaps and Buzzcut released a track titled '*I like girls*', where Ghaps rapped about coming out of the closet. She knew her parents or family were never going to listen to the track. It was a tight one-minute track, part Mumbai English and part filmi Hindi. For the beat, Buzzcut sampled '*Aaj ki raat*' from the *Don* soundtrack—the

Shah Rukh Khan version. He added a thick bassline under it, with a lot of broken beats strewn around. Ghaps retired the name MC Ghapaghap and uploaded the track as Gayatri—'*I like girls*' (Prod. by Buzzcut).

When the YouTube upload crossed 1000 views, Buzzcut and Ghaps, for the first time in their music-making lives, felt that this could be their scene. To just produce complete tracks and upload them to YouTube, and not worry about the rap and hip-hop scene around them. Over the next few weeks, Buzzcut and Ghaps released one more track titled '*Juhu beach pe sunset*'. They got twelve new followers on Instagram and two new subscribers on YouTube. Three of their Insta followers were girls. One of them had a display picture taken at a Pride parade, where she was kissing another girl.

Utkarsha was the first person apart from Ghaps and Buzzcut to notice all of this activity. She had been the only follower and fan they had for the longest time. Then Raveena joined. Utkarsha stalked the girls who started following Ghaps on Insta, checking their every update. When Nikunj asked Fehmida to follow Ghaps and Buzzcut, she refused outright. She said she couldn't follow an account with less than 1000 followers. She said the same thing about promoting Buzzcut and Ghaps's track: 'It has to cross 10K views at least. It would affect my social media ranking badly otherwise.' Nikunj thought that was fair. Buzzcut and Ghaps didn't care enough to be offended. Perhaps the older Ghaps would've tried to make Nikunj dump her, but the new Ghaps was a different woman. In fact, she was Ghaps no longer. She was the calm and collected Gayatri—out there to spit truths and split rhymes.

To celebrate crossing 1000 views, Buzzcut and Ghaps told Nikunj that they should plan an evening out with the girls. They had never hung out as a group. They couldn't go anywhere other than the mall (because of Fehmida's restrictions), so they decided to watch a movie at the multiplex and grab dinner at one of the pubs. This was the first time alcohol was involved in a hangout with the girls.

Raveena didn't stop bugging Fehmida about TikTok, not that Fehmida minded. She was happy to impart knowledge. They even made a TikTok together, which Raveena posted on her timeline. It was the Raveena–Karishma–Karishma–Raveena dialogue from *Andaz Apna Apna* (where Raveena played Karishma and Fehmida played Raveena).

Utkarsha spent the entire evening giving Ghaps the stink eye. But for some reason, Ghaps was immune to it. She was so comfortable in her own skin that it was almost like she was full of herself. She continued to ignore all the hints that Utkarsha was mad at her, and put her arm around her like everything was normal. Utkarsha kept shaking her arm off her.

At some point after the movie, when they were sitting at the pub, eating chicken lollipops and guzzling beer, Utkarsha got drunk. She had repressed everything; she wanted to scream at Ghaps and had drowned her anger in beer. By the time she finished her third beer, she lost all patience. Utkarsha slammed her glass down and walked out. Ghaps just stood there, watching her walk away. Buzzcut nudged Ghaps to get up and follow her. She snapped out of her trance and chased after Utkarsha.

Utkarsha exited from the back gate of the mall, which opened into the parking lot. She found a giant SUV to stand behind and cry. Ghaps reached for her, and she pushed Ghaps away. Ghaps asked her what happened, and Utkarsha screamed, 'Which of the three women followers on Instagram are you flirting with?'

'What?' Ghaps didn't know what had hit her. This new avatar of Ghaps didn't care enough about followers.

'I know what you are planning. You are going to get it on with one of your fans, just like you did with me. I was your first fan!'

Ghaps realized then that while she had been busy questioning her existence and writing songs, the one person she had taken for granted was Utkarsha. She thought their relationship was solid and that Utkarsha would be there for her no matter what. She knew Utkarsha picked up the slack in their relationship. In fact, it was the only reason Ghaps could focus on herself.

'Why would I hook up with one of my fans? I've never seen you as my fan!'

'Then? What am I to you?'

'You're my girlfriend! I love you!'

'I am sure you've said I love you to those other three followers also!'

'Which three followers?'

'Oh, don't tell me you don't see the notifications on your phone!'

'I really didn't! The last few months, everything has changed, I have changed—'

'And now you have no place for me in your life?'

'No, no, I didn't mean it like that!'

'C'mon, Gayatri! You're going to chase one of those new followers. Accept it.'

'Why should I?'

'You weren't even there for me when I told you Papa was in the hospital.'

Ghaps fell silent. Before she could find the words to apologize, Utkarsha said, 'I've made up my mind. Don't call me or message me for a few days.'

'Will we be fine?'

'You tell me.' She turned and walked away towards a rick. Ghaps just stood there staring. She had never felt so out of words as she did that day. She had never had to apologize to anyone for behaving shittily with them. Mostly because she had never had anyone rely on her like Utkarsha did. She watched Utkarsha get into the rick and leave. She messaged Buzzcut and Nikunj on the WhatsApp group, telling them that Utkarsha had left and she was going home too.

The evening out wasn't disastrous for everyone, though. Raveena had an epic time. Before Raveena met Fehmida, she thought that she was jealous of Fehmida's success. But after meeting Fehmida, she realized that she hadn't been jealous.

She was just afraid that Fehmida would turn out to be a stereotypical social media influencer (read: bitch).

When Buzzcut dropped Raveena home that night, she clung to him—feeling his entire body against hers. She asked him to stop in one of the streets where someone had broken a couple of streetlights to provide a shelter for lovers.

Raveena got off the bike and kissed Buzzcut. He counted his heartbeats in his head as he dived into the kiss. It was the perfect track that lasted for 3 minutes at 160 bpm. When Buzzcut got home, he put all that romantic energy that his body had generated during that kiss into the most hypnotic track he had ever made. He sampled parts of the old Dimple Kapadia–Jackie Shroff song '*Tera naam liya*', added a beat, sound effects and an aalaap Ghaps had secretly recorded on her phone outside a classical music school in her neighbourhood. There was also the constant hiss of rain in the backdrop of '*Raveena's kiss*'. Both Ghaps and Nikunj tripped on it when he sent it to them on WhatsApp.

Nobody saw Ghaps for a few days. On Christmas morning, Buzzcut and Nikunj received a voice message. Ghaps had written a poem called '*Utkarsha*'. She had rapped it and sent it to them. It was very moving, and it had some actual verbal gymnastics that were a rare feature in Ghaps's raps. This time, Ghaps even sang a few lines for the chorus.

Later that day, Ghaps went to the Vodafone store where Utkarsha worked. She took a few numbers from the queue machine and waited until she was assigned Utkarsha as her customer care executive. Utkarsha nearly jumped off her high chair as she saw Ghaps approaching. Ghaps walked up to Utkarsha's desk, put her phone down with the poem open on the screen. Using the screen as a teleprompter, she performed 'Utkarsha' for Utkarsha. Tears started flowing down her cheeks. She grabbed Ghaps by her elbow and dragged her out to the lane next to the store. The two hugged and kissed. Ghaps told Utkarsha that she was her only one. She had had a crush on Utkarsha even before Utkarsha started following the rap Instagram account. She didn't fall for Utkarsha because she was a fan.

Having had too intense a week, Ghaps made a plan with Buzzcut and Nikunj to forget about their lives—the good parts as well as the bad—and focus their energies on dominating a server on PUBG. This time, instead of hanging out at the park, the three of them met at the small godown office-studio. It had a sofa and a desk (with a laptop) and a chair. Ghaps had bought the best pair of speakers that she could afford to amp the studio feeling up.

This was the first time the three of them did not ration their drinks. They knew that if they ran out, all Ghaps had to do was step out into the godown and pick up one more bottle. Buzzcut wasn't able to centre himself for some reason that day, so he kept dying early in every game. Without him flanking Ghaps and Nikunj, they died somewhere in the top ten but never got to the top three as they had wanted to.

With his head swimming in wine, Buzzcut put his phone down and lit a cigarette, 'I'm not playing.' Ghaps and Nikunj shrugged, and continued. Buzzcut started playing with his phone instead. He put on his earphones and listened to the folder of mp3s with stuff made by Ghaps and him. Halfway into crushing weed to roll a joint, his phone played Ghaps rapping '*Utkarsha*'. Midway into that rap, he pulled his earphones off, put the weed down and waved at Ghaps and Nikunj. 'I just realized what has been fucking with my head all this while!'

'What?'

'Nothing. You guys continue playing, I'll tell you in a few minutes.'

Buzzcut finished rolling a joint, lit it and started working on the laptop. He smoked the joint all by himself and absent-mindedly held on to the butt for over half an hour. When he was done, he waved that joint-*wala* hand in Ghaps and Nikunj's direction.

'Chutiya, that joint is over.'

'I'm not passing you the joint. Here, listen to this.' He pulled out his earphones from the laptop and plugged in the speaker's aux cable. The phone played a version of '*Raveena's kiss*', which had Ghaps's '*Utkarsha*' rap placed over it.

'What's going on? I can't make out anything. Is something off with the beat?'

'No, no, no! I get it ...' Ghaps jumped up, 'It's just off the beat by a little. I can rap it a little differently, fix a few words, and we have a track.'

Ghaps shut down the PUBG app on her phone and opened the Notes app, on which she had written '*Utkarsha*'. 'Play "*Raveena's kiss*" again, without my vocals.' Buzzcut obliged. Ghaps started rapping lines, correcting them in the app and asking Buzzcut to play it again.

Nikunj did not understand head or tail of what was going on. At some point, he passed out on the couch. It was a little past 4 a.m. when he woke up. Ghaps and Buzzcut were still at it. As soon as Nikunj's eyes opened, the two of them waved him to shush. Ghaps had a mic in front of her, which was plugged into the laptop. And she broke out into this beat-perfect version of her poem that fit like it was designed to be coupled with Buzzcut's track. As soon as the track ended, Nikunj fell back into a deep sleep, assimilating the track as a part of his dream.

In the morning, Nikunj woke up and went home. Buzzcut and Ghaps decided to get some air and some beer after a night full of Red Bulls and Thumbs Ups, sleep deprivation and pot. They were in the park at 8 a.m., sitting on top of the jungle gym, drinking beers as everyone around them jogged, worked out, or did yoga. Buzzcut called the studio manager and took the day off. The studio manager did some natak, but ended up giving them the night slot for a bag of weed and the promise that Buzzcut would DJ at his son's birthday party.

Ghaps called the shop and asked them to sambhalo for a day. Buzzcut and Ghaps grabbed breakfast at an Irani cafe and then returned to the studio. Ghaps did one more take.

It was a more relaxed take, like she was talking to someone sitting on her couch. And all she could do was rap and dance about it, whereas she'd much rather be kissing that someone on the couch. This was the take they were most satisfied with.

They transferred the final cut of the track to their phones, and asked Raveena and Utkarsha to meet them for lunch at the mall. They asked Nikunj if they could borrow his and Fehmida's home at the mall for a listening party. Nikunj asked Fehmida, who approved of sharing their space with near and dear ones.

Buzzcut and Ghaps took Raveena and Utkarsha to the secret spot, sat them down and made them listen to the track separately on their phones. They took mental notes of every expression on Raveena and Utkarsha's faces. When the girls jumped forward to hug them, our friends just went in for a kiss. After the two kisses lasted the length of the entire track, both Ghaps and Buzzcut rushed back to the studio to make final tweaks based on the facial feedback (in more ways than one) that they had collected from Raveena and Utkarsha.

Ghaps changed a few words around. Buzzcut broke some beats, added a moment of silence in the middle of the track, which picked up with Ghaps singing the chorus all by herself before the instruments kicked in once more. The final version was uploaded on YouTube, Soundcloud, Instagram and Facebook as '*Gayatri: Utkarsha's kiss* (Prod. by Buzzcut)'. The track got over 30,000 views on YouTube in a week.

23

Nikunj told Kalpeshbhai and Kashmira bhabhi that maybe they needed to spend some time apart. Their brains had started thinking alike, and perhaps this separation would give them some perspective. So Nikunj did not leave his bed after that call. Instead, he watched the house in motion around him. He saw Nikita get ready and leave for office. She gave him a tapli before she left. To which Nikunj groaned, 'Go away, no!' and covered his head with the blanket. Nikunj had to get up to see Vipulbhai off in Kalpeshbhai's car to Juhu. (Vipulbhai wouldn't go until Nikunj personally went to the driver and said, 'Please drop my father for his treatment.') Nikunj returned to being supine as he watched Shardaben, Toral bhabhi and Ilaben run in and out of the kitchen and the house. Sometimes, Shardaben and Toral bhabhi went to their own homes, and returned with a missing ingredient, utensil or mixie vessel. Sometimes they would take a vessel full of stuff that needed to be cooked on their stoves at home and bring it back once it was done.

Nikunj avoided looking at his phone or replying to any of the messages after that morning call with Kashmira bhabhi. He didn't want to look at his phone because he knew he would unlock it if he saw Fehmida's message notification. Then he would feel forced to respond. Then he would feel guilty for not responding to the others, and he would end up replying to everyone. So instead, Nikunj took a nap. By the time he woke up, the lunch hour had passed. There was nobody at home. He called up Ilaben, who gave him the following updates: 'We are at Shardaben's house. We are trying to master ringna nu lasagna for Italian night. Rotli-shaak-daal-bhaath are in the kitchen. Keep the leftovers in the fridge. Okay, bye.'

Nikunj grabbed lunch and turned on the TV. There was a news report on the dual attack of the gastric epidemic—a constipation crisis in ISRO Colony in Bhopal and a simultaneous wave of extreme gas in Matunga, Mumbai. People in Matunga were constantly feeling queasy or nauseous, and all their burps and farts smelled lethal. Traffic had been rerouted from either side of Matunga because of rumours of people fainting due to the deadly farts. The news channels and the government spokespersons had finally started tacitly acknowledging that this gastric crisis was no longer an issue only of Mumbai and Maharashtra but a national issue. Nikunj saw yet another opportunity to prove himself as better than Dr Garodia. He was going to help people without the motivation of money—completely and totally selflessly.

He finished lunch, looked up Matunga on Google Maps and saw the list of 'places near you' below the map. He called the first place on the list and asked if the person who picked up if they were suffering from indigestion or if someone around them was affected by the epidemic. Nikunj told them he was calling from the Municipal Corporation's Health Department. As soon as he was on the line with someone affected, he used his powers to help them feel at ease. After helping thirty-eight people, he felt a little better about himself.

Then he turned off the TV, stepped out for a smoke, but walked to a farsan shop and got a samosa pao instead. After the snack and a Kashmiri soda, he grabbed a smoke. On his first big burp, he realized that he was really missing his college days—the days when he didn't have to do anything. He wanted to be at peace, but the rest day wasn't helping him like he had hoped it would. He was still itching to help people. It was the first day in months that he didn't have any appointments and he didn't know what was happening in the lives of the people he loved.

So he replied to all the messages on his phone, telling people he would get back to them. Fehmida had sent him the link to her latest TikTok video. She had participated in the TikTok eye-roll challenge. The idea was to perform different eye-rolls to different song lines. Fehmida's video, which got the highest number of hearts as compared to anyone on the trend, had a line from '*Choli ke peechhe kya hai*': '*Begum bagair Badshah kis kaam ka? Badshah bagair begum kis kaam ki?*' She rolled her eyes up as she matkaaoed them left to right to the beat. It made Nikunj smile and, for a moment, forget everything else happening in his life. This is what she did all the time. Every time Fehmida messaged him, sent him a selfie or a TikTok video, it would make him smile—widely and openly. This was the first time Nikunj had smiled in the entire day. He sent her a Boomerang of him exhaling smoke, and then went home and went to sleep.

When he woke up next, Ilaben stood above him, shaking him awake. 'What is wrong with you?' She didn't know how to deal with his behaviour. This was the first time since college that she saw Nikunj behave like he had no care in the world. It confused her because she knew he had a lot of concerns.

'Nothing, I just need some rest.'

'Aevu kaai no hoy, you have to keep working. Or you'll become lazy and lose your life. Don't you know what happened to Hardikbhai? I've told you. He stopped working, saying he will take a break. Now look where he is. He is helping his wife run her khichdi stall!'

Ilaben was genuinely confused. Someone had replaced her brand-new working son with an older version. The one who used to hang around a lot, mostly supine somewhere in the house, like a screensaver until someone nudged the mouse and woke him up. Just like an old computer, Nikunj was finding it difficult to connect, and he made noisy modem noises on being nudged by Ilaben.

'Leave me alone, no! Go, Shardaben and Toral bhabhi are waiting for you in the kitchen.'

Nikunj was annoyed by his mother's intrusion, and he couldn't go back to sleep after that. He returned to the khau galli and got himself another samosa pao. This time, he went to the gola-wala outside the park and got himself a nimbu pani. He finished the nimbu pani with a cigarette while counting rickshaws on the road. He only got up and left after he saw ten go each way.

24

The international evening kitchen that Ilaben, Shardaben and Toral bhabhi started became a huge success. They were fulfilling a couple of hundred orders every day. The lunch tiffin service stayed on as their flagship product, but they switched things up by locking the number to the first fifty orders. The ladies wanted to have comfortable mornings now that they were making a lot more money in the evenings. Toral bhabhi took beautiful pictures of the food they made and made posters on Canva for their dinner service. The posters also featured a portrait of all three chefs. They sent these posters to all their customers on WhatsApp, along with the menu for the week.

Nikunj had slept through most of the second half of the day. Somewhere in the evening, Toral bhabhi's seven-year-old nephew poked Nikunj awake. 'My dadi says that if you sleep in the evening, your mind will be taken over by rakshases. They are most powerful at sunsets.' Nikunj ignored the advice and closed his eyes anyway. When he properly woke up, Ilaben and gang were sending out the second batch of dinners with the two rickshaw-walas hired for this purpose. Ilaben was in a celebratory mode because they had cracked the aubergine lasagna. They had also thrilled themselves to bits by adding small bottles of pink lemonade with their orders. It was Shardaben's idea. 'Just pour a couple of drops of Mapro rose syrup in nimbu pani. Done!'

Nikunj didn't remember ever seeing Ilaben as satisfied as she had been for the last few weeks. It had everything to do with the culinary empire she had created for herself in a radius of about two kilometres around their house. Watching Ilaben glow in the aftermath of a successful day, Nikunj smiled for the second time that day. It made him feel he could discuss his work problems with her.

After the final batch of tiffins were sent out, the three ladies poured three glasses of pink lemonade, and raised a toast: 'Three cheers! Hip-hip! Hurray! Hip-hip! Hurray! Hip-hip! Hurray!' Then they drank the lemonade and disbanded. It was Shardaben's turn to provide customer support that night, so she took the work phone they had bought specially for the tiffin service and went to her place. Toral bhabhi picked up the food she had packed for her home that night and waved goodbye. Ilaben closed the door behind Shardaben and Toral bhabhi, and came straight to Nikunj.

'Will you get out of bed and go do something? Go meet Gayatri or Buzzcut!'

Nikunj just sat up, but didn't say anything.

Ilaben sat down next to Nikunj. 'What happened?' She ran her hand through his hair.

The Gholte-Butalas were not ones to discuss each other's problems or pour their hearts out. In fact, the only person who aired every little problem he had and whose problems were dissected and solved as a family was Vipulbhai. Nikunj and Nikita discussing their lives with each other made them the first pair of siblings in three generations of Gholtes and Butalas to get close to each other. Else, the only problems that mattered in any house were the problems of the eldest person under that roof.

So Nikunj felt a little strange talking to his mother about the problem he was facing with Kalpeshbhai, 'I have this one patient, you know Kalpeshbhai ...' Nikunj told Ilaben everything. Everything that made any kind of sense to him. She did not disbelieve any part of the story—not even the part about Kalpeshbhai's golden turd. She did, however, make that face she made whenever someone talked about things that weren't to be discussed out loud under her roof. The digestive and excretory system was one of those things. You were allowed to fart as loud as you had to, it just did not need to be addressed. Unless, it was Vipulbhai's digestive system. The status of his digestive system was to be announced whenever something moved in his stomach. (And, of course, each time he did this, Ilaben made that exact face and shook her head.)

Ilaben sat silently for a few moments before she said, 'Are you feeling guilty?'

'About what?'

'About taking their money but not being able to help? Do you think your powers won't be able to help them?'

'I don't know. I don't think I'm feeling guilty, though.'

'Good. The day you start feeling guilty, that day you say sorry to them and leave the job. It's not fair to them if they are being treated by someone who is not confident himself. That will be like swindling them. We don't need to do things jaema aapdu mann kharab thaaye.'

'I sometimes do feel like I am becoming Dr Garodia.'

'Bobdi band kar! There is no way you are like Dr Garodia. The day I feel you have become like Dr Garodia, I will slap you myself.' She made Nikunj laugh by saying that. It was a laugh of relief. Ilaben paused for a moment and continued like they never stopped talking about Kalpeshbhai, 'You know, I think emne koi ni najar laagi chhe. You don't believe in all this, but these things are real. You know, Shardaben's elder sister, Hansaben? She is very good at removing najar. Do you want me to call her?'

'No, ya, Aai! This is such a serious problem! The last time I went into a dream to make him poop, and you are saying try jhaad phook!'

'No, no, no jhaad phook. Hansaben uses nimbu and water and mirchi and some spices only. No jhaad phook.'

'That's not what I'm saying.'

'I know, but I believed you when you said that you went into somebody's dream and made them do … that. Then believe me once, no? I have never asked you to believe in anything. This is for someone else's good that I'm saying, no? Not yours.' Ilaben really knew which buttons to push. It was true, though. She had never asked Nikunj to believe in any god or temple. Nikunj read some atheist things on Facebook when he was in his first year of junior college, and that made him wonder if he was one. That day onwards, he stopped believing in anything that Ilaben and Vipulbhai had made Nikunj and Nikita do since they were kids—go to the temple, sit for poojas and havans, feed the cows and crows, and more. When Nikunj stopped, Ilaben didn't say anything. Vipulbhai tried to scold some sense into him, but Aai discouraged him. It did hurt her, but all she said was: 'You may not want to understand why we need to be dharmik, but that's okay. I won't try to convince you because you will say ugly things about what we believe in. I don't want that bitterness in this house.' Nikunj didn't understand what she said that day. He was ready to fight and regurgitate all the social media philosophy he read. But the truth remained that she had allowed Nikunj to believe in whatever he wanted to.

'Okay, tell me more about jhaad phook.' He resigned, and she resumed moving her fingers through the back of his hair as she told him the story of Shardaben's younger sister's son, Tapan.

Tapan had started acting differently after Shardaben's mother passed away. He did nothing but sit around all day on the sofa that his grandmother sat on. Then he started saying words that he had never learnt himself, but Shardaben's younger sister had heard her mother using these words and phrases. He even started peeing sitting down. So she freaked out and called the eldest sister, Hansaben. Hansaben's prognosis: Their mother's spirit had not left the world yet and had possessed Tapan. Hansaben caught a train from Amdavad and went straight to her younger sister's house in Ghatkopar. There, she did some reverse magic, and suddenly the boy felt differently. That day he was still dazed till he went to sleep at night. The next day, Tapan woke up and was back to being normal. He threw the same tantrums that he always threw, sneaked extra biscuits out of the kitchen and refused to go to school. Shardaben went to visit him during that period. She had been so distraught for those two–three days that Toral bhabhi and Ilaben gave her the bare minimum work, and nothing with knives after she cut herself once because her mind was on poor Tapan.

'Now do you believe me?'

'Okay, okay, I'll talk to Kalpeshbhai and Kashmira bhabhi. I'll ask them if they want to try jhaad phook.'

That made Ilaben feel happy and virtuous. Everything had gone right with her day, from inventing aubergine lasagna to helping her son. She pulled his ear playfully, ruffled his hair and said, 'Good boy.'

Nikunj, of course, wasn't planning on bringing this up with Kalpeshbhai at all. He felt that as Tatti Raja, it felt stupid to say, 'My mother helped me with my homework.'

25

Nikita came home earlier than usual that night. Contrary to precedence, she wasn't in any kind of rage. She usually came home early only when someone had pissed her off at work, or when she got mad at Abhimanyu about something. Nikunj followed her into the kitchen to ask her what was up.

'Nothing,' she said.

'You're home early.'

'So?'

'Nothing, you sure?'

'Yes, nothing. You want some cha, or you want to annoy me some more?'

'No, I won't take any cha.'

Vipulbhai had also returned home. He heard the cha conversation and asked her to make some for him. As soon as Ilaben entered the living room, he made a fuss about eating international food every day. Whenever he went on a long rant, he forgot to speak in complete Gujarati sentences and burst out into some Marathi. '[In Marathi accent] Dinner madhe [to Gujarati accent] rotli-daal-bhaat-shaak [to Marathi accent] milael [to Gujarati accent] ke?' After years of being a Marathi manoos married into a Gujarati family, this was all that remained of Vipul Gholte's Marathi roots. Other than his kids calling their mother 'Aai'.

Ilaben listened patiently and then snapped back as soon as he paused for a breath. 'There are leftovers from morning. Aam pan, you eat snacks for lunch at the new clinic. Might as well have rotli-daal-bhaat-shaak once a day, no?'

'Don't talk about the new clinic. Keeda padey Mansukhbhai par!'

'What happened? What did he do?'

'He hurt everybody's feelings and insulted their faith. Can you imagine Mansukhbhai's guts? He insulted Dr Garodia!'

'Who? What? When? How?' Nikita, who promptly zoned out the minute Vipulbhai started talking about the clinic, felt her ears perk up as soon as the words 'insulted Dr Garodia' fell on them.

Ilaben set the table as Vipulbhai dramatically narrated all that had happened at the new clinic. He first gave everyone a crash course on how Mansukhbhai Patel was Damuben Patel's builder son. Damuben had become besotted with Dr Garodia, much like any of the regulars at the clinic. Using her influence, Dr Garodia had converted the Patel outhouse into his clinic-cum-residence. He had even gotten a swing installed in the centre of the living room. That was his singhaasan. It was polished with ittar every day. The outhouse became an ashram of sorts, where all kinds of ill came for the miracle cure but stayed for the company.

The latest was that Dr Garodia was making a crown for himself. He had collected enough gold from his more affluent patients. He told them that the gold would help him channel the right energies to help heal them faster. To complete the crown, he asked Damuben for a centrepiece diamond—large enough to ring all sorts of bells in the Patel household. It was a montage of twenty-eight spit-takes from eighteen members of the Patel family, their seven servants and three drivers. (For some reason, everyone was drinking water or tea whenever and however they heard about the diamond demand.) None of Dr Garodia's patients found the demand irrational.

Nikita broke into tumbling laughter. Ilaben was worried for the Patel family. She prayed for a moment for their well-being. Her prayers were not required because this is what happened next in Vipulbhai's story.

After Dr Garodia told Damuben about the diamond, she thought for a minute. Then she asked him, 'How many months will you be able to cure my arthritis in?' He said, 'Five times lesser than what it was originally going to take.' Damuben nodded and told him that she would let him know in the evening. Dr Garodia was confident that he was going to get a diamond. As soon as Damuben left, he wore the diamond-less crown and continued to treat patients. Damuben did not come for the next two treatment sessions. She told Dr Garodia that some urgent family matter had come up. Dr Garodia told Vipulbhai that she must definitely be arranging for the diamond.

In the evening, when Mansukhbhai returned from work, he invited Dr Garodia for dinner. Vipulbhai followed Dr Garodia to the dinner, hoping he would get to witness Dr Garodia's moment of glory. When they got to the dining table, the entire house was empty apart from two servants serving food. Mansukhbhai sat at one end of the long dining table. Dr Garodia's and Vipulbhai's plates were served at the other end of the table. There was no food on their plates.

Mansukhbhai started eating. He even licked his fingers between morsels. For a few minutes, the only noise you could hear was of him licking his fingers, breaking a papad and the clanking of his spoon. Dr Garodia started sweating in the air-conditioned dining room. Then one of the servants came and placed a printed A4 paper on one side of Mansukhbhai's plate. Mansukhbhai started listing account numbers and their amounts in rupees, asset names and their present-day worth in rupees. Dr Garodia grew paler and paler. 'I will give you your diamond tomorrow. But I will come to the outhouse to see a miracle. Any miracle you choose. You don't even have to tell me beforehand. Cure somebody. Move something. Ae tamara par chhe.'

That was when Vipulbhai realized what had just transpired. This was not a dinner invitation. It was a threat. It was an affront to Dr Garodia's greatness. He was about to say something when Dr Garodia stopped him by placing a hand over his hand. Then he gulped once, made a brave face and told Mansukhbhai, 'Of course, of course. You will see the magic happen as soon as the diamond will touch my skin.'

Vipulbhai beamed at his family members around the table as he finished his report on what had transpired between Mansukhbhai and Dr Garodia. 'It was amazing! Dr Garodia just gave it back to him! Sometimes, you know, rich loko ne paisa ni charbi chadhi jaay! They forget how to treat a pure man, a true man.'

Vipulbhai was confident of seeing a miracle the next day. Nikita, meanwhile, hadn't eaten a single morsel of her dinner. She still had the first forkful of brinjal lasagna sticking on to the fork, gaping at Vipulbhai. Ilaben sneaked in a couple of giggles in the kitchen before making a straight face and returning to the living room. Nikunj was genuinely afraid that Dr Garodia was going to perform a miracle and blow everyone's mind. The fact that he had made a crown for himself had to mean something.

That night before going to sleep, Nikita asked Nikunj, 'Why do you look like you're the one who is being tested and not Dr Garodia?'

'What if he manages to perform a miracle?'

'Yeah, right.'

'You don't know half the things about the half-medical community. Sometimes they can perform real miracles.'

'We'll see tomorrow.'

'Also, can you believe it? Aai, who believes that Dr Garodia is a fraud, is asking me to try jhaad phook on Kalpeshbhai?'

'You mean like Hansaben's jhaad phook?'

'Yes, exactly.'

'So what's wrong with that?' Nikita had been immersed in the feminist blogosphere and memes in the spare time she had at work. It made her sharper and more ruthless in the way she cut through the crowd and stood out in the office.

'What do you mean? What's wrong with that?'

'No, seriously! Why do you men think that you can do everything by yourself? Here a family of women are trying to help you, and you're acting like Dr Garodia!'

That hurt Nikunj. 'Fuck off!' He returned to watching TV.

'You fuck off.' Nikita turned over, sent Abhimanyu a good night kiss on a video message, plugged her earphones in, and went to sleep.

Nikunj frantically switched to a news channel to catch an update on the gastric epidemic. Anna Nagar in Madurai faced severe acid reflux, which even led to ulcers in some of those affected. Nikunj had to do the one thing that he thought he did which was most unlike Dr Garodia—cure people for free on the phone. He couldn't have just gone to sleep for two reasons—he had slept all day, and he had to redeem himself in his own eyes after being compared to Dr Garodia.

The next morning, he called Kashmira bhabhi and asked her about jhaad phook. Kalpeshbhai, who was on speakerphone, shouted from the back, 'Yeah, obviously, we haven't thought about homegrown jhaad phook!'

'What?'

'Ignore his tone,' said Kashmira bhabhi gently. 'He is in so much pain that all his words are coming out in a painfully sarcastic tone.'

'So you want to try jhaad phook?'

'Yes, yes! We really hadn't thought of trying homegrown jhaad phook. We had always directly called the professional tantriks and babas thinking they would be at a higher level.'

Nikunj told Ilaben and Shardaben about it. Ilaben had already told Shardaben, who had already called Hansaben, who said she would be in Mumbai as soon as her grandson's unit tests were over.

26

It was the second morning in a row that Nikunj cancelled on Kalpeshbhai. Instead, he went with Vipulbhai to see Dr Garodia's big miracle. When they got to the Patel bungalow, the gates were shut. This was something new because the entrance to the Patel bungalow was always kept open, as a matter of principle. That day, the guards had been letting in only some select people and cars. None of Dr Garodia's patients or their families were on that list. A small crowd had gathered outside the bungalow. All kinds of stories and rumours were floating around about what must have happened inside. Nobody was actually asking for an explanation from the guards. There was no fear of this mob turning violent because a majority of them were severely ill or temporarily/permanently disabled.

Vipulbhai waded through the crowd, exchanging pleasantries and collecting gossip. When he was refused entry by the guards, he shouted, 'Arre! What are you saying? Just yesterday I was having dinner with Mansukhbhai. Tell him Vipulbhai is here.' Once the crowd heard him confidently challenge the authority of the guards by namedropping, he became the unanimously elected class monitor for the picnic.

'Arre! Dr Garodia is going to perform a miracle today for Mansukhbhai. He will need at least my assistance.' The rest of the crowd confirmed this by nodding in sync. According to them, Dr Garodia would obviously need assistance from his right-hand man.

'Nobody called Dr Garodia has ever lived in this bungalow. This is the Patel family bungalow. You all must be confused,' one of the guards said flatly.

Vipulbhai asked if he could go meet Mansukhbhai or Damuben. He was told that he would have to take an appointment with their business manager first. Somebody from the crowd had already gotten their business manager's information. Vipulbhai called the business manager, who told him that there was no appointment available for six months. Vipulbhai returned to the crowd. He told everyone to wait, he was going to call Dr Garodia on his personal (basically, Dr Garodia's wife's) number. The phone was switched off.

Diksha bhabhi, Rameshbhai's wife, found Vipulbhai and Nikunj, and asked them to come with her to her car. Rameshbhai sat in the back with his grill-encased leg stretched across the seat. He said they had dug around for some information, but right next to Mansukhbhai's bungalow wasn't the safest place to discuss the details. So they went to the Juhu Shiv Sagar, where they spoke over rava masala dosas. Rameshbhai had called some of the richer people in the disability circuit until he found one connect to Mansukhbhai—a lady who was in the same kitty party group as Mansukhbhai's wife. She told Rameshbhai the full story.

The previous night, after Dr Garodia had agreed to perform the miracle, he returned and met Mansukhbhai without Vipulbhai. Dr Garodia fell to Mansukhbhai's feet and told him he would leave the outhouse immediately. Mansukhbhai didn't budge. He insisted on having Dr Garodia perform that miracle. Dr Garodia stayed saashtaang at his feet. A few minutes later, Mansukhbhai walked to the nearest chair and sat down. Four men showed up. All of them looked like *CID*'s Daya except all of them were a different shade of brown. The United Colours of Daya were introduced as a security agency that ensures a certain kind of action is taken on behalf of those who hire them. Mansukhbhai asked Dr Garodia to get up. 'I know you have a house in Baroda. These young men will help you put your things on to a truck, put you in a car and drop you to your house in Baroda. Then they will stay in Baroda to make sure you do your job.'

'What will be my job?'

'Nothing. You will do nothing. I know all your aankdaas; you have enough to send your son to the US to study, and enough to feed you and clothe you till he starts earning.'

'Okay, vadil, I am very grateful to you.' Out of habit, Dr Garodia couldn't stop there. 'If you need any treatment, call me. I will do it for free!'

Mansukhbhai made a 'get lost' gesture with his hands. Dr Garodia was escorted back to the outhouse. A truck was called and just like that, Dr Garodia and his family were moved to Baroda overnight. Nobody knew anything about

Dr Garodia's past, so nobody knew where in Baroda to go looking for him.

Rameshbhai wept as he finished the story. He had called many people in Baroda already to see if someone had moved into their neighbourhood overnight. But Baroda was a big city. Rameshbhai was sad that there would be no more picnics. The clinic and its community would disband, and they would never see each other again. At least they would still have the WhatsApp group that Rameshbhai and Vipulbhai had started. The group already had 'We Miss You, Dr Garodia' messages and images in which Dr Garodia had been photoshopped next to gods and goddesses. Vipulbhai was stumped. Rameshbhai asked, 'What will we do now, Vipulbhai?'

Vipulbhai banged his palms down on the table, spilling everyone's sambhars a little, stood up and proclaimed, 'Mansukhbhai is such a gunda! All these rich people are rich in money only, not sanskaar! Who drives a god-like doctor away from his patients? Aapdu beeju kon chhe aa duniya maa Dr Garodia sivaay?' Rameshbhai and Diksha bhabhi agreed and sat up straight on hearing Vipulbhai's words. Nikunj cringed and just wanted to run away. He didn't know what to say. Anything he said would be countered by Vipulbhai with 'I know you just hate him.'

Diksha bhabhi said, 'We're seeing if we have any influence that connects us to Mansukhbhai directly.'

Rameshbhai continued, 'Someone bigger than Mansukhbhai, someone who Mansukhbhai will listen to.'

'We can ask for a favour. I am sure they will understand if all of us patients show up in support of Dr Garodia.'

After they were ushered out of Shiv Sagar for not ordering more, the three of them spent some time calling the older core group from the clinic days. It was much smaller and tighter than the new crowd that had filled the Patel outhouse. Rameshbhai, Vipulbhai and Diksha bhabhi tried hard to poison the community against Mansukhbhai Patel, but some of the calls backfired. Some had lost their faith in Dr Garodia entirely. Others were too scared to get into a panga with 'these builder types'. Then there was the worst kind: The ones who were convinced that Dr Garodia must have done something wrong against the Patel family. 'Why would he throw out Dr Garodia for no reason?' After each call, the three of them would discuss the picnic member they had just called and rate their loyalty to Dr Garodia.

The entire scene got a bit too much for Nikunj. He wanted to leave, but didn't know if he should leave Vipulbhai alone. He also couldn't be the only one to know of this development, so he called Nikita. At first, she said she was in a meeting and would call him later, but the moment Dr Garodia's name came up, she asked Nikunj to hold. She told her meeting that 'an urgent family matter has come up'. Then she locked herself in the cabin as everybody else left and asked Nikunj for every detail he knew. As Nikunj narrated the story he had just heard, she kept saying, 'I can't laugh, I can't laugh, but this is so funny. People think I am on a serious family emergency call in here. I can't wait to tell Aai about this.'

'I hope Papa will be okay after this,' Nikunj said at the end of the story.

'Oh, he will be. He will just have to find something else to do than be a free assistant to a conman.'

'I'll wait till they are done here, then drop Papa home before getting to work.'

'Are you mad? Just go, do your work. Papa will be fine. He can get an auto for himself.'

Nikunj wasn't convinced. He stayed with Garodia's three angels and watched them enlist seven more patients to storm the gates of the Patel bungalow. The next day, all of them gathered once again outside the Patel bungalow demanding an audience with Mansukhbhai. They were told that Mansukhbhai wasn't home. Vipulbhai became the trope of that old man in Bollywood movies—the one who keeps kaatoing court ke chakkar with his trusted sidekick, Rameshbhai (and his wife Diksha bhabhi) in this case, but finding no justice. Garodia's Angels continued their mission on WhatsApp, hoping that one day they would be able to reverse this gross injustice that had happened with Dr Garodia and his patients.

A few nights after Dr Garodia's banishment, Fehmida's family had gone to an uncle's house. The uncle had suffered a heart attack and was in pretty bad shape. Fehmida told her parents she would stay home and take care of the house, in case they needed food or something. As soon as she sent them off, she called Nikunj up. 'We have never watched a late-night show together.' She wanted to hold hands with Nikunj, rub them together, and play with his warm fingers on the last row seats of the air-conditioned movie hall. Nikunj, who was sitting, waiting for the next patient, jumped up and said, 'Yes! Tonight! Find a show after 11.'

That night, after the movie, Fehmida and Nikunj took a stroll through the empty, shutdown mall. She talked about all her TikTok videos, and he told her everything that happened in the day. They stopped at stores, which still had some of their display lights on. They put their faces and palms against the glass, and peered into the shops. The glass still smelled of Colin. Then, for the first time ever, they walked with their hands in each other's back pockets. A few minutes into the back-pocket walk, Fehmida pulled away from Nikunj, pulled her phone out and said that she wanted to make a TikTok video. She wanted to participate in the #SiameseTwins challenge. It was where people dressed and wore make-up to look exactly like each other, and made a TikTok video. She pulled out a wig that looked exactly like her hair, clip-on hoop earrings and a copy of her own top, which was two sizes bigger, for Nikunj.

'Put these on.'

'What? No!'

She ran her palm over his cheek, pulled it and smiled into his eyes. That smile told Nikunj that this could be the beginning of the silent treatment if he didn't comply.

'Okay,' he resigned to his fate, 'give it to me.' He looked around once to make sure nobody was watching them, followed Fehmida's orders and let her dress him. 'Now what?'

'Now, come here.' She gestured him to her side, with her hand in place at the height of his back pocket. Then they resumed the back-pocket walk around the mall with their cheeks pressed to each other. They were conjoined twins. Fehmida had not chosen a soundtrack for this video. She wanted it to be a vlog about conjoined twins, who were out shopping at a mall and were ranting about how none of the clothes were designed for them. 'That would look so good on us! But alas, narrow-minded people have made it only for themselves.' They walked past stores, which had their lights on, where Fehmida flipped the camera front and back to give the audience a look at the wares in the middle of their rants.

Every now and then Fehmida gave Nikunj extra sideboob. The smell of her perfume was already driving him out of his mind—in a good way. She didn't feel very differently from him. So she stepped away as soon as she stopped filming. They walked around quietly for a little while until she finished the video and set it to upload. 'Drop me home, like a real date.' She kissed Nikunj on the cheek, the same one she had licked for the #LickAStatue challenge and the one that was connected to her when they played #SiameseTwins. Nikunj felt that from that moment on that cheek of his was forever hers.

The words 'real date' made Nikunj call for an Uber, rather than take one of the million rick guys waiting right outside the mall. For Fehmida, this was really important because this was the first time she was going to be with someone on her way home. All her commutes back home had always been alone, even after having a good time with Nikunj at the mall.

She was aching to stretch the perimeters of their relationship to include bits of the outside world. While they waited for the Uber outside the mall, she put an arm around his elbow and took selfies like 'real couples' do. Nikunj smoked with his free hand, and took turns gazing at the Uber app and her face. His chest swelled up, and his shoulders broadened. Not knowing what to do with that feeling, he kissed her on the side of her head.

27

Nikita and Nikunj celebrated Dr Garodia's banishment with a quarter of Old Monk and a joint. Nikunj finally told Nikita everything about Fehmida. He even told her about the 'real date' they went on. He didn't tell her about their TikTok challenges together though. Nikunj felt those were a bit too risqué to describe. He did tell her about their secret corridor, however, and how they pretended to live-in when they were there. Then he showed her some of the selfies that Fehmida had taken of the two of them and sent to him for memory purposes. (Nikunj wasn't allowed to take selfies of them or even pictures of her because he 'didn't have the eye for it'.) Nikita's eyes widened, and she laughed a little. 'She's so out of your league! I mean, she's just so beautiful and cute. What did she see in you, ghochu!' She slapped the side of his head. 'I want to meet her.'

'I don't know … It's too soon.' In truth, Nikunj really wanted them to meet and get along as fast as possible. But in his head, a kiss had become the most critical next big step in their relationship. As if it was a boss fight that unlocked future levels of the relationship game. Also, Nikita had taken her own sweet time with Abhimanyu. They had even made life plans together before she brought him home to meet everyone. 'You didn't even let me meet Abhimanyu separately before Aai–Papa. Why should I treat you any different?'

'That's because you're a ghochu and I'm awesome.'

'Sure, sure.'

'To love!' Nikita raised her glass. When they clinked their glasses together, she grabbed him by his chin and made him look into her eyes. 'Always look someone in the eye when doing cheers! Else it's seven years of bad sex.'

'Eww ... I don't want to know about your sex life.'

'Good, you won't if you do cheers right. Once again! To love!'

After Nikunj looked her in the eyes as she toasted them, they spoke some more about Dr Garodia, Fehmida and Abhimanyu. Then Nikita put the empty bottle of Old Monk into her bag to throw it in a public dustbin on her way to office. They couldn't let Ilaben or Vipulbhai spot it in their dustbin. Even if they missed it, their building sweeper-cum-garbage collector was on good terms with Ilaben, Shardaben and Toral bhabhi. The four of them exchanged gossip often. That friendship grew as the amount of garbage coming from the Gholte-Butala house increased with the growth in business. Ilaben deemed it necessary to give her some extra money for their home only. So she would definitely snitch on Nikita and Nikunj if she found an Old Monk bottle in the garbage coming out of their house.

Nikunj thought that they'd all be better off now that Dr Garodia was gone. But a week after his banishment, he managed to re-enter their lives even while absconding. The Gholte-Butala household became the central office for the 'Bring Dr Garodia Back' movement. They even got a huge printout of Dr Garodia's face on a flex and mounted it in the living room. Garodia's Angels (Vipulbhai, Rameshbhai and Diksha bhabhi) presided over the meetings. Many of Dr Garodia's patients visited them to discuss elaborate plans to find the good doctor and bring him back. Someone even brought along a private investigator, but Garodia's Angels decided that that was the tedhi ungli if seedhi ungli didn't work. They wanted to try legit ways to reach Mansukhbhai first and appeal to him before nosing around in his business with Dr Garodia. There were other channels employed in the finding of Dr Garodia. Every member of the Bring Dr Garodia Back movement called everybody they knew in Baroda and asked if they had seen anything suspicious, or any new neighbours who looked like the Garodia family. Photos were circulated on WhatsApp, particularly one where Dr Garodia sat on the throne-swing with Mrs Garodia and their son standing behind him. In that picture, Dr Garodia was wearing the diamond-less crown too. None of these efforts had yielded any results.

Between Ilaben's business and Vipulbhai's new hobby, the house was always full of people. Nikunj whined about how it felt like they were living on some railway platform, waiting for a train that was never going to arrive. Even the bedroom was occupied. Unfortunately for Nikunj, Nikita got ready and left before the masses arrived. He would've enjoyed watching her destroy everything in her path if her routine was disturbed by any of them.

Finally, Shardaben's elder sister found the time and arrived from Amdavad to help Kalpeshbhai. Hansaben looked exactly like Shardaben. She wore the same pastel saris, the same round bindi. Except, she was bigger in every other sense. She was literally Shardaben's 'big' sister. Hansaben wore her hair in a bun, whereas Shardaben wore it in a single plait. Outside of the differences in their size and hairstyle, they looked exactly like Gujarati matryoshka dolls. Hansaben carried theplas for all the households that were now a part of the larger culinary empire family—Ilaben's family, Toral bhabhi's family and, of course, Shardaben's.

In the car, on their way to Kalpeshbhai's, Hansaben opened another steel dabba of theplas and a small bottle of atthaanu. She put a few on the lid and passed the lid to the driver and Nikunj in front, asking them to have some. Both declined. The driver smiled and told Nikunj that Kalpeshbhai's grandmother behaved exactly like this whenever she arrived from their town in Gujarat. To Hansaben, it was obvious to bring theplas if you were taking a long ride from Mulund all the way to Juhu. According to her, 'You can reach Amdavad in that much time.' There might have been a little truth to her claim.

Hansaben asked Nikunj about Kalpeshbhai's illness. He told her everything that he knew and then she asked him about his 'motions problem'. Once again, he told her everything he knew.

When Hansaben, Shardaben and Nikunj reached the Sheth house, Hansaben wasn't at all awestruck by the magnificence and the whiteness of the house. Shardaben kept flexing her core muscles, and checking out various nooks and corners of the house to find one dirty spot. Hansaben spotted Kalpeshbhai's father watching the news in front of the television and offered him some theplas, saying, 'These are straight from Amdavad.'

'Then I must take one!' He loved it so much, he took away the entire dabba, and asked the servant to get plates and serve the theplas to everyone.

Satisfied, Hansaben, Shardaben and Nikunj had tea with Kalpeshbhai's father, Kalpeshbhai and Kashmira bhabhi. To show respect to Amdavad's finest, the Sheth kitchen served their own claim to fame: thalipith and dahi-sambhar ni chutney with ginger–mint–lemongrass–cardamom tea. Hansaben spoke about how jhaad phook had been happening in their family for generations. She spoke of their aunt, Chhotiben, who got possessed by Mataji every Navaratri. And of their grandmother, who had once rid an entire village of evil spirits, which harassed the villagers after a tantrik's spell blew up under a peepal tree. Once the tea was had and the stories petered to a stop, in the awkward silence, Kashmira bhabhi asked, 'Shall we begin then?'

'Yes, yes, of course. Have you kept everything ready?'

'Yes. Come with us to our room.'

Nikunj wheeled Kalpeshbhai to their bedroom. Kashmira bhabhi went to the kitchen and got the thali with everything that Hansaben had asked for—cumin seeds, salt, red chillies, mustard seeds, a steel lota and a piece of red cloth. Hansaben asked for a tava to be put on the gas and pre-heated while they performed the first part of the ritual.

She filled the lota with water and dropped a nimbu in the water. Then she tied the lota with the red cloth and did Kalpeshbhai's aarti with it. She asked Kashmira bhabhi which was the east corner of the room, and put the lota in that corner. Then she took all the masala and held it in a fist over Kalpeshbhai's head. She closed her eyes and said some words. After she was done, she walked straight to the kitchen and put the masala on the hot tava. It sizzled, and there was a lot of smoke, but the smoke smelled like someone had sprayed the house with air freshener as opposed to making everyone gack and cough.

Nobody understood what happened, but it gave Shardaben and Hansaben goosebumps. They leaned into each other and muttered something in Gujarati that nobody else understood. Then Hansaben darted to the east corner and opened the lota to check on the nimbu. It had turned into a shining silver nimbu! 'The one possessing Kalpeshbhai is not a ghost or an evil spirit! It's a divya shakti! I don't think I am pious enough for this ritual. I'll have to call my masi from Amdavad.'

Hansaben and Shardaben's maternal aunt, Chhotiben, was perhaps the most badass matriarch in the mystical and half-medical circles in the Gujarati community of Mumbai and Gujarat. Chhotiben was famous for being possessed by Mataji every Navaratri, where, in a trance, she would reveal truths and make predictions. Whatever she said while in the trance had always come true. Every Navaratri, their entire extended family visited her to have at least one bhog ka meal with her. They got a sense of direction about wherever they needed to go. Vipulbhai and Ilaben had been planning to take Nikita and Nikunj to Chhotiben ever since the business partnership between Ilaben and Shardaben had evolved into a sambandh.

28

Two days later, Chhotiben arrived with the swagger of an aunt who walked in on her nieces playing ghar-ghar. She was short and round. She looked like the Russian doll that would fit inside Shardaben (who, in turn, could fit inside Hansaben). Chhotiben didn't bring any theplas. Instead, she was served the theplas that Hansaben, Shardaben, Ilaben and Toral bhabhi had made for her (and the tiffin service). Chhotiben took one bite, chewed it and rolled it around her mouth. Then said, 'These are too thick. Butter paper jeva paardarshik hova joiye.' According to her, they were not translucent enough. 'Although your atthaanu has come out fantastic this year!' That made Shardaben and Ilaben happy.

Once again, in the car ride to Juhu, Nikunj narrated everything he knew about Kalpeshbhai to Chhotiben, Hansaben (who was listening to the story for the second time) and Shardaben (who was listening to the story for the fourth time). Both Hansaben and Shardaben had become excellent listeners of this story. They gasped and nodded at all the right places.

On reaching Kalpeshbhai's, Chhotiben walked in like she belonged there. There was a glowing radiance about her which made everyone do a double take as she passed. In fact, upon her arrival, Kalpeshbhai's parents sought her out and touched her feet. She blessed them. Chhotiben did not want to waste time tasting food or tea before the ritual. She straightaway asked Kashmira bhabhi, 'Aapde sharu karye?'

Chhotiben's version of the ritual involved a branch of neem leaves. She pulled out a chair and sat next to Kalpeshbhai's head. She put her hands on his forehead and muttered something. Then she slapped Kalpeshbhai with the neem leaves. The neem leaves dried and withered right there in front of everyone. On seeing this, Chhotiben backed off a little. 'This is a strong shakti.' She hadn't expected to fail, so she had not asked for the ingredients of the next step to be kept ready. But she had no choice now but to move on to the next step. She turned to Kashmira bhabhi and said, 'Can you get me one onion, chopped into two, and two cloves of garlic?' Chhotiben tucked a garlic clove and half an onion under Kalpeshbhai's armpits. 'You are going to get a fever in a few minutes. That will allow the shakti inside you to speak with us directly. If you are feeling sleepy, please drift off.'

Within twenty minutes, Kalpeshbhai was running a high fever. His body turned red-hot. Chhotiben expected him to drift off into a trance so that the divya shakti could surface and communicate with them. When that didn't happen, Chhotiben pulled the onions and garlic out from under his armpits. She put a hand on his forehead, looked into his eyes and said, 'Are you there? Can you hear me? Come out and talk to us! Why do you possess this body?'

Suddenly, Chhotiben shook like she was being electrocuted. Her hair, which was in a tight bun, unravelled and fell around her head. She entered a trance, and her body started moving in circles on the chair. Her eyes rolled up. 'There is so much light. I can't see anything.' She spoke through the trance before she started whipping her hair back and forth. 'I can't see anything, I can't see anything …' And then she passed out.

Kashmira bhabhi called for tea for everyone as they waited for Chhotiben to wake up. When she woke up, she repeated the same words. 'I couldn't see anything! I don't believe this. This has never happened to me before. This must be some very powerful divya shakti at work!' She touched Kalpeshbhai's feet and asked for forgiveness from the divya shakti. Kalpeshbhai's fever had broken, and he had started to sweat profusely. Chhotiben asked Hansaben and Shardaben to ask for forgiveness too, and pray to the divya shakti to not harm their families. The three of them apologized and left. They didn't even stay for lunch, saying that they had caused enough problems already. Chhotiben, especially, looked terrified. As soon as they left, Nikunj called Ilaben to ask her to ask Shardaben what had happened, since she wasn't telling him anything—no matter how much he asked as he walked them to the car. Chhotiben had zipped her mouth shut with a glance. Shardaben really wanted to tell him everything. In her own words, Nikunj's mother was like a sister to her, they were like family.

When Nikunj got home, Ilaben had already received the lowdown from Shardaben. But they were running late on the delivery of spaghetti with paneer, corn and spinach balls. The YouTube video had promised them that the balls would break exactly like meatballs. But they didn't. So it took the ladies a little while to improvise a version that would. (The secret was corn starch.) All their customers got their dinners at 10 p.m. that day. The culinary trio decided to not charge any of their customers for their delayed shipment. 'Who wants to listen to their kitch kitch? They'll only whine once if it's for free. Else, each call would be long and loud. Who wants that?' Ilaben explained her decision to nobody who asked, which was Nikita and Nikunj. Nikita simply nodded, took her plate and went to the bedroom to video call Abhimanyu, who was in Gurgaon for a vendor meeting.

Vipulbhai, Rameshbhai, Diksha bhabhi and three other members of the Bring Dr Garodia Back movement were having an intense and quiet discussion in the living room. Ilaben put an end to their day's play by handing everyone a plate of spaghetti and paneer–corn–spinach balls. They stopped talking and got busy stuffing their faces.

By the time Ilaben got done with the dinner service and cleaning the kitchen, it was a little after 11 p.m. in the night. The "Bring Dr Garodia Back" movement disbanded for the day. Shardaben and Toral bhabhi packed dinner for their families and left. Before leaving, Shardaben nodded at Ilaben to tell her to pass on to Nikunj what she had told her. Ilaben thanked Shardaben with a glance that assured her that she would tell him everything.

Ilaben and Vipulbhai retired to their bedroom. Nikunj sneaked out, got stoned, and returned to following the poopocalypse on the news. Ilaben walked out of the bedroom in her nightie. Something about that made both Nikita and Nikunj get up. Once Ilaben went to the bedroom, she never stepped out until the morning, not even to pee. Those four-six hours were all hers. The only other time she slept was half an hour in the afternoon after finishing the lunch deliveries and before starting with the dinner service.

'Ubhi kaem thai gayi?' Ilaben asked Nikita to sit, hugged her face, kissed it and asked her about her day. Nikita told her it was alright. Ilaben didn't believe her and said, 'Don't worry, it will get better tomorrow.' Nikita smiled. Then Ilaben looked at Nikunj, 'Saambhal, will you come press my legs? I can't fall asleep.'

In the bedroom, Vipulbhai was writing 'Ram Ram Sita Ram, Krushna Krushna Radhe Krushna' in his notebook. It was a habit he had formed when he was a child. In his childhood, he had learnt about this form of bhakti from old people in the park. So ever since he was a child, he had his own notebook to write that line 108 times every night before he went to sleep. Ilaben sat with her back against the headboard of their bed, with a jap-mala (made of 108 beads) in her hand. Nikunj sat next to her legs and started pressing her calves.

'So Shardaben said that Hansaben is afraid that you have gotten involved with a divya shakti. Chhotiben told me that we might have to do jhaad phook on you too. There must be some effect of the divya shakti's magic on you also.'

'I don't want to do any jhaad phook and all. I am fine.'

'Niku beta, they could sense disturbing energy around you also. Please try and understand. These women are saying this from a place of care and love.'

'No means no, Aai. I help so many people every day. I know how this works, and I will figure out Kalpeshbhai on my own.'

'Tu saambhalto kem nathi? They asked me if I could ask you to stop treating Kalpeshbhai. You might invite the prakop of the divya shakti into your life!'

Nikunj found this ridiculous. Instead of helping Kalpeshbhai, the ladies had created another monster for Nikunj to deal with—the fear that something was wrong with him. He felt that this whole jhaad phook had been a bad idea from the beginning.

'Are they saying Kalpeshbhai is cursed by a divya shakti or the power protecting his illness is a divya shakti?'

'They are saying that they can't see anything because of the divya shakti. They don't know anything. They don't even know if what is possessing him is good or bad. They are afraid that an attempt to remove it might backfire, hurt Kalpeshbhai or all of us. It has already affected you.'

'How? I am healthy and fine only!'

'Tu saambhaltoj nathi! You have been stubborn like this since you were a child. We are saying this for your good only.' She leaned forward and ran her free hand through his hair and on to his face. 'You are such a sweet boy; you are helping so many people. What if something happens to you?'

'Nothing will happen to me!'

Vipulbhai listened in on the entire conversation, but didn't say anything till he finished writing his mantra 108 times. As soon as he was done, he used his pen as a bookmark, closed his book and put it by the bedside table. 'Why didn't you tell me this was a constipation problem? It is sad that the only person who could help you is missing, probably kidnapped.'

'Papa, we know for a fact that Dr Garodia hasn't been kidnapped.'

On seeing where the conversation was going, Ilaben concentrated on her jap. Vipulbhai thought that Kalpeshbhai's family was influential enough to bring Dr Garodia back. He only had to engineer it through his son.

'We don't know that. We only know what we have heard through others. Nobody has seen or heard from Dr Garodia in all these days.'

'Okay, okay. You are right.' Nikunj didn't have the energy to argue with a fanatic. 'I just don't want Dr Garodia's help. I think I can handle this on my own.' There was a part of Nikunj that was tempted to try Dr Garodia with Kalpeshbhai, but he dared not mention that because he didn't want to enable Vipulbhai's obsession any further. Nikunj, Ilaben and Nikita thought that it was only a matter of time before Vipulbhai and the rest stopped thinking about Dr Garodia, and moved on with their lives.

'Maybe if Dr Garodia can cure Kalpeshbhai, then he can ask Mansukhbhai to get off Dr Garodia's back. I'm sure the two rich Gujaratis from Juhu know each other well.'

'All rich Gujaratis don't necessarily know each other, Papa! And Kalpeshbhai is my patient, and I will take care of him.'

'Beta, sometimes you have to be humble and accept that there are higher powers than yourself.'

'You watch and see how I take care of Kalpeshbhai without Dr Garodia's help.'

On hearing Nikunj's tone, both Ilaben and Vipulbhai frowned. And so did Nikunj's heart. He needed to stop comparing himself to Dr Garodia, but there was always a little voice somewhere in some corner on the right side of his brain telling him how similar to Dr Garodia he had become. Especially with Kalpeshbhai as a patient—someone who Nikunj couldn't cure but continued to take money from.

For the next few days, Ilaben reminded Nikunj to try jhaad phook for himself. She kept asking him if she should rent a taxi to Amdavad. She wanted him to ask for Hansaben's and Chhotiben's forgiveness, and ask them to rid him of all the ill energies threatening his well-being. Of course, they wouldn't make the trip to Mumbai for someone as healthy as Nikunj. He would have to show responsibility for his own spiritual health.

29

In February, the weather was on the verge of breaking into a summer rash, but it was still bearable. The Mumbai Pride parade had just happened, and Fehmida had seen a lot of posts from it on Instagram, YouTube and TikTok. Fehmida had the last face-paint idea of the season before everything got too sweaty.

She made a TikTok video where the audio was the voice of a small child saying, 'Colour colour, warm colour, cool colour, bright colour, wrong colour, right colour, which colour do you want?' For the video, she bought the seven coloured backdrop roll from Amazon. She painted her face with food colours that contrasted with the backdrop. She added a flip camera transition at every comma in the audio.

This video was her magnum opus in terms of social media popularity. It was in more than eight 'coolest/hottest 100 emoji, 100 emoji, fire emoji' TikTok video compilations. Because it was connected to the Pride parade, a queer film festival in Bangalore used it as their opening video. The brand manager of Ramolac Paints was queer, and was attending the film festival. When he saw the video, he reached out to Fehmida, asked her if they could buy her concept for a video they wanted to make for Holi. Fehmida didn't know what to do, so she told him she was busy and that she'd call him back.

The first person she called was Nikunj. The first thing she said when he picked up was: 'I will need to open a bank account.' She didn't want her parents to find out she was about to make money as a social media influencer. That would then mean she would have to disclose her social media presence and show her TikTok account to her parents. She wasn't ready to find out how they'd react to her videos. She was afraid they would take her phone away. Her parents were happy that she was keeping busy without leaving the house. If she became too outgoing, it might become challenging to find a groom for her, they reasoned. They hadn't started looking for a groom for her because her brother had to get married first.

So Nikunj and Fehmida made a plan. Nikunj took a day off from Kalpeshbhai, and went with Fehmida to help her open an account at the bank branch where Buzzcut's dad worked. When she was told that the ATM/debit card would be sent to her home, she freaked out. Thankfully, because of Buzzcut's dad, they were able to convince the guys to hold on to her ATM/debit card at the branch. She would have to collect it by showing a photo and address proof.

The first non-white lie that Fehmida told at home was that she was going to the mall. Instead, she took Nikunj with her to a meeting with the digital agency that worked for Ramolac Paints. Usually, she only lied by omission when she told them she was going to the mall. The impression her family had was that she was going to be walking around the mall all alone, window shopping (or actually shopping), and grabbing a bite to eat by herself. All that had changed so much since Nikunj had become a part of her life.

While Nikunj and Fehmida waited in the all-glass conference room, they were spotted by Abhimanyu. This was one of the agencies that Abhimanyu's company dealt with. He was there for a meeting too. He waved at them from across the cubicles, excused himself from his team and popped into the all-glass conference room. 'Arre, Nikunj! Bhai! What are you doing here?' The display of familiarity felt a little alien to Nikunj. And he couldn't fake his emotions in front of Fehmida. She held that power over him. So the half-hug got a bit awkward. Nikunj told him why they were there. Abhimanyu shook his head and delivered a very familial scolding about not calling Nikita. 'Your sister is the best account manager I know! You should get her involved in this meeting.'

Nikita, obviously, proved herself to be the champ that she was. Nikunj had no idea what Nikita's work personality was like. And there was only one word to describe what it was like: Baller. He heard the switch between 'Didi' and 'baller' on the phone itself. When he called her, she asked him if the call was about a Dr Garodia update. (That was the only time ever that Nikunj had called her at work.) The moment he told her it was about Fehmida, Nikunj heard her postpone another meeting with the 'family emergency' excuse. Nikunj gave her the full update, and as soon as it was established that this was a business consult and not a brotherly update, her voice switched from a loving lilt to crisp and staccato. She told him to put her on speakerphone. 'Hi, Fehmida, Nikita here,' she began. 'I don't have time to discuss the strategy with you this time. Do you trust me?'

Fehmida hesitated and looked up at Nikunj, then she said, 'Yes, I trust you.'

'Good, then send me screenshots of your Insta and TikTok profiles, and let me do the talking through the speakerphone. You don't have to say a word. Got it?'

'Got it.'

'Nikunj, this means you too.'

'Yes, of course.'

The meeting lasted exactly seventeen minutes and forty-eight seconds. For the first ten minutes, Nikita, Nikunj and Fehmida heard everything that the two brand managers sitting on the other side of the table said. Then for the next seven minutes and forty-eight seconds, Nikita spoke, and it was like listening to a symphony. By the end, Nikita asked Fehmida to shake hands with the two brand managers. She then proceeded to kick the two brand managers out of their own conference room and asked them to give her a few minutes with 'the talent'. Nikita got Fehmida Rs 2.25 lakh for the concept and a promise to deliver five more colour-related videos over the next three months for Holi. She then fake-scolded Fehmida (just like Abhimanyu fake-scolded Nikunj) for not monetizing her social media presence already: 'Look at those numbers, girl!' The lilt in her voice was back, and she was out of business consultant mode. All Fehmida had to do was to return the next day to sign the contract and collect her first cheque.

Fehmida looked like she had gotten stoned for the first time. She was frozen till they got out of the building and got into an Uber. Nikunj was afraid that people might think he was forcefully taking her somewhere. Fehmida's body fell loose the minute they sat into their Uber. She raised her hands and squealed so loudly that the driver slammed his brakes and gave Nikunj an acrimonious look. Fehmida started laughing. The driver shook his head and gave Fehmida a look that said, 'You girls of today!' On the cab ride to the mall, Fehmida couldn't stop talking about the meeting. She referred to Nikita as Didi, just like Nikunj did. In her words, 'Didi slayed that meeting!' With each 'Didi', her pitch grew higher and higher.

Fehmida and Nikunj celebrated the success of the meeting by watching each other eat popcorn during a movie. Her lipstick, her hoop earrings and her irises reflected the light of the screen, and Nikunj was lost in them. His irises were dark—they disappeared in the darkness of the movie hall. She wanted to go looking for her eyes in her eyes. They were so lost in each other's eyes that they forgot why the hero was mad at the villain in the movie they were watching.

If Nikunj didn't have patients waiting and if Fehmida hadn't run out of the plausible amount of time that could be spent at the mall alone, the two of them would have hung out longer and made at least one TikTok video. Nikunj secretly hoped she would use him to make another video that day. He carried that longing to be seen by Fehmida's phone camera lens as he went about his day.

30

A few days later, Nikunj had just returned home from meeting patients in Kurla. Nikita was already inside, watching the Korean drama that Fehmida had recommended. She had a remote dangling off her hand and her wrist dangled off her knee. Everything about her was on the edge of being dragged into a cyclone of emotions. Before Nikunj could wake her up from her edge-itated state, he heard Vipulbhai call him from the bedroom. 'Niku beta? Is that you?'

Nikunj washed his feet and went into the bedroom. Vipulbhai was doing his nightly writing ritual. He continued writing and asked Nikunj to sit next to him till he finished. Nikunj sat there for a couple of minutes, and then told his father that he'd change and come. Once again, Vipulbhai gestured for Nikunj to sit down as he focused on writing the names of the gods. A couple of minutes later, Nikunj tried to get up again, and Vipulbhai made him sit down again. That was when Ilaben spoke up: 'Just sit down for two minutes! He will finish and talk to you.'

On hearing Ilaben's tone, Vipulbhai hurried to the end of the page, put his book away and said, 'Dikra saambhal, I know you don't like it when I say this, but I am not saying this out of any selfish interest …'

'Saying what?'

'See, I am only telling you this because it's for Kalpeshbhai's benefit. I have no selfish motive in telling you this.'

'Telling me what?'

Vipulbhai was sure he couldn't establish the fact that he wasn't acting out of selfish interest any further. 'You should ask Kalpeshbhai to try Dr Garodia's treatment. You know how he cured my constipation so quickly. There are many people like this whom he has helped with muscular puncturopathy. That time there was Kantaben's son who stopped doing tatti for four days. She forced him to come to Dr Garodia.' Kantaben herself had been going to Dr Garodia to cure her cataracts. She didn't want doctors to poke around her eyes like she had seen them do in a cataract surgery video. 'He has cured many people like this. He is a good man with only intentions of serving the public.' Kantaben had to get the surgery eventually.

'Who else has he cured, Papa?'

'That time he cured my constipation after I hadn't done tatti for a week! Remember?'

'You were also on a lot of laxatives that day, Papa. It could be anything.'

'You have lost your faith, dikra.' He turned sideways, put his hands on Nikunj's, looked into his eyes and said, 'Sometimes, you have to put your ego aside to help other people. I understand that you don't like Dr Garodia, but I have seen him do magic with his fingers … Trust me, I am only saying this because that poor Kalpeshbhai has been suffering for so long.'

'It's under control, Papa.'

'That poor man hasn't suffered enough already? Yet, you didn't ask Dr Garodia for help. This is not the son I raised.'

Vipulbhai's blackmail played rather well on Nikunj's mind, which was like a minefield of tiny comparisons between Dr Garodia and himself. He wondered if he was keeping Dr Garodia from helping Kalpeshbhai because he saw him as competition. Vipulbhai's accusation made him ask himself if he had started seeing himself as Dr Garodia's equal. Finally, that little voice from the corner on the right side of his brain won. 'Okay, okay, I'll talk to Kalpeshbhai tomorrow.' And the little voice whispered a follow-up, 'After all, Dr Garodia and I are in the same line of work.'

'Exactly! Both of you help people.'

By Vipulbhai's logic, a commitment becomes stronger the longer that a silence is maintained between the committer and the committed-to after the commitment is made. It becomes a bond of karma, a bond of dharma in Vipulbhai's head. So when Vipulbhai was finally satisfied with the length of the silence that followed after his son agreed to his proposition, he asked Nikunj to get some sleep—but not without dishing out a final taunt to his broken integrity. 'Tomorrow, you're going to be doing something good.'

When Nikunj left the bedroom, Nikita was still in the same position. The channel had changed though. For some reason, she was watching the news about the indigestion crisis in Hooghly-Chinsura, a small city to the north of

Kolkata. He plonked himself next to Nikita and nudged her. 'What happened? Bad day? Should I roll a joint?' He wanted her to be done with her problem, so that he could bitch about succumbing to Vipulbhai and bringing Dr Garodia back into their lives. He wondered if she'd laugh at him or be mad at him.

'Nothing. I don't want to talk about it. Why are you looking like someone punched you in the gut?'

'Nothing. I don't want to talk about it.'

'Yes, you do. I sense what you're about to tell me will affect both our lives.'

'I have to try to bring Dr Garodia back. I am going to take his help with Kalpeshbhai.'

'Oh, great!'

'I don't know what to do.' Nikunj told her the whole story.

Nikita didn't have an option but to agree with the choice he had to make. 'Try once with sincerity, just so that you can say that you didn't disrespect Papa. It's not necessary that Kalpeshbhai will agree to see the fraud. Even if he does, Dr Garodia does have a successful track record with constipation. So what's the worst that can happen? Kalpeshbhai won't poop. Then Dr Garodia will go back to his life in exile.'

Nikunj realized then that he was more afraid of Dr Garodia succeeding than he was of Dr Garodia failing to make Kalpeshbhai poop. If he succeeded, then he would become a legit god in the eyes of his believers. He would be resurrected in their lives, and those who turned their backs on him or doubted him would have to eat their words. He felt foolish for having his priorities all wrong. He was becoming more like Dr Garodia by not giving the doctor a chance. He didn't want to talk any more about this strategic forfeit in his battle against Dr Garodia (which was only in his head).

To Nikunj's mixed fortune, Kalpeshbhai agreed to the idea. But he was worried about how hesitant Nikunj sounded when he pitched the idea. 'Nikunj, you know that there are no bad ideas. We have to try everything.' So Nikunj told him the full story of his relationship with Dr Garodia, including the latest scandal at the Patel residence.

Kalpeshbhai and Kashmira bhabhi laughed because they had met many such doctors in the last two decades. 'They're all experts in medical fields that nobody has heard of. But let's try this Dr Garodia once.' He said he would talk to Mansukhbhai and find a way to get Dr Garodia back into the city for a day. Apparently, Mansukhbhai and Kalpeshbhai went to school together. They had drifted apart in the years since Kalpeshbhai's illness. While Kalpeshbhai became occupied with his rigorous search for a way to heal or at least poop, Mansukhbhai had taken over his dad's job of running the family business.

31

Nikunj hoped that Kalpeshbhai wouldn't follow up on the Dr Garodia conversation. But he also wanted to prove that he was a better human being than Dr Garodia. That he put his patients first, and therefore, was giving the doctor a chance. Kalpeshbhai brought up Dr Garodia when they next met. He decided to make an effort to meet Mansukhbhai in person to ask for the favour.

Kalpeshbhai and Mansukhbhai had gone to the same school. They had even played cricket together after school. They weren't the best of friends or anything, but they were two from the few in their circle who didn't do their engineering or medicine and move abroad. They stayed back in Juhu to be with their family, to run and expand the family business. In fact, Mansukhbhai was the first non-family member to reach the hospital when the news got out (through the house-help network) that Kalpeshbhai had been struck by a sudden illness. Of course, they were just Kalu and Manu then, and hadn't yet become their respectable, fully named older selves.

Kalpeshbhai asked the Sheth family's right-hand man, Gulabbhai (who was the son of Kalpeshbhai's grandfather's right-hand man, Phoolchandbhai), to call

Manojbhai (Mansukhbhai's right-hand man) and fix a meeting. Apparently, Mansukhbhai did not even blink before he said yes to the meeting. He was surprised by this blast from the past. A part of him wanted to go to Kalpeshbhai's house and slap him, but maturity and stature prevailed over emotions.

The day of the meeting was fixed. The venue was Mansukhbhai's outhouse, the same outhouse that had once been the clinic. After kicking out Dr Garodia, the Patels had held a havan to cleanse the outhouse. According to the family, such weaknesses in the armour protecting the family from harmful things—such as manipulators like Dr Garodia or any major illnesses—came only when the gods or the spirits of their ancestors were angry at them. The Patels also hosted a feast at the temple, where 108 beggars were fed to their heart's content. They also gave each beggar one set of clothes each.

Nikunj helped Kalpeshbhai into his wheelchair. Kashmira bhabhi helped with the straps that held him up. They got into Kalpeshbhai's modified car, which had a ramp and enough space to fit a wheelchair in the back. Nikunj sat in front with the driver. Kashmira bhabhi sat with Kalpeshbhai in the back. The couple was on a silent trip down a melancholy memory lane. They were going to meet people they hadn't seen in over a decade.

Vipulbhai wanted to go with Nikunj and Kalpeshbhai to Mansukhbhai's house to act as Dr Garodia's advocate.

According to him, nobody was better qualified to represent Dr Garodia than him. Nikunj, though, was afraid that Vipulbhai's devotional speech would irk Mansukhbhai and that might throw a wrench in the works. So Rameshbhai, Diksha bhabhi and Vipulbhai held a prayer circle for the Kalpeshbhai–Mansukhbhai meeting to go well.

Mansukhbhai stood outside the bungalow with his wife to welcome Kalpeshbhai. Mansukhbhai asked Nikunj to move away and helped Kalpeshbhai off the van himself and wheeled him into the house. Kumud bhabhi, Mansukhbhai's wife, hugged Kashmira Bhabhi tightly. That classic Bharat-milap scene had its own history. Almost all of Kashmira bhabhi's friends got married and left Juhu for either Walkeshwar or America. So when Mansukhbhai got married, and his wife moved to Juhu from Walkeshwar, she had no friends in the area. Kashmira bhabhi and she became friends quickly. Their evening thing was to power-walk together all the way to Sahakari Bhandar, get a pani puri and power-walk back. Nikunj was glad that Vipulbhai and the Bring Dr Garodia Back movement weren't around to ruin this reunion.

Nikunj followed the four of them to the outhouse. Mansukhbhai looked at him suspiciously. Maybe he remembered seeing him there with Vipulbhai or his face reminded him of Vipulbhai's. Of course, Mansukhbhai did not know the reason for which Nikunj was there with Kalpeshbhai and Kashmira bhabhi. 'Do we need extra help? I can help you if you need anything,' said Mansukhbhai.

'Oh, please. This is Nikunj. He is the Tatti Raja, and he is helping me with my illness. I need him here for today's discussion.'

'What's a Tatti Raja?'

Kalpeshbhai explained. That worried Mansukhbhai a little. He looked Nikunj up and down. 'I hope this is not one of those babas and frauds who is taking advantage of your illness?'

'Trust me, he is not. We have actually tested his powers,' Kalpeshbhai assured him.

Tea and snacks were served in the living room of the outhouse once the five of them settled. Mansukhbhai patted Kalpeshbhai on his back. 'This is only the beginning.'

Kumud bhabhi added, 'Haan, Kashmira, today you two are not leaving without eating lunch.'

More pleasantries and some memories later, the two of them were back to being Manu and Kalu. Kumud bhabhi fished out an old photograph of Kalu and Manu together with three or four other boys, all of them dressed in cricket whites. The picture was taken in the open area of the Patel compound, on which the outhouse was constructed ten years ago. Manu and Kalu told stories about their cricket team, which doubled as a mango thief team in the raw mango season. They jumped compound walls across bungalows in Juhu and stole mangoes. They were the terror of the neighbourhood. Once Mansukhbhai's grandfather had caught them red-handed with all the mangoes. He beat them all with their own cricket bats. He then told Mansukhbhai, 'There are so many mangoes here at home, and yet you want to steal them!'

'But, bhabhi,' explained Mansukhbhai, 'stolen mangoes taste the best!'

Kalpeshbhai laughed. 'Sometimes we stole enough to last us the full season! We just gave them away.'

'Either to beggars or the cooks in our own houses to make fresh pickle out of.'

Once the laughter faded, Manu asked Kalu, 'What is it that you wanted to talk to me about?'

Kalpeshbhai and Kashmira bhabhi exchanged a glance. Then, Kalpeshbhai said, 'We want to talk to you about Dr Garodia.'

'Not you too, Kalu! Not after we've just become friends again after all these years.' Apparently, the Bring Dr Garodia Back movement had been successful in creating *dum* in Mansukhbhai's nose. They had reached out to him through many channels.

'You have to understand, Manu, I wouldn't ask if it wasn't of utmost importance.'

'Do you know how many people have called me about Dr Garodia? These are some really important people.'

'I know, I'm sorry. I didn't know how to talk to you about this. The full story of how Dr Garodia played with Ba's emotions is really shocking. If I were in your place, I would have ghasitoed him from here to Baroda behind a car. But I have come to a point in my life where I really must try Dr Garodia's treatment once. All these years of trying to find a way to poop have led me here.'

'We don't expect you to understand this, Manubhai, but please consider this once,' Kashmira Bhabhi intervened.

'But, bhabhi, he really is a fraud. You don't know how he *gidgidaooed* in front of me once I exposed him. That's the worst! He knows he is a fraud!'

'Not entirely, from all the stories I have heard. Dr Garodia has a way with constipation.'

'I heard those too, but most of them fall apart once you poke them further. My security team did a thorough job. They said that the patients were all under the influence of laxatives when he "cured" them.'

'Don't send us back with empty hands, Manu. We have come here with a lot of expectations.'

'At least give us his address in Baroda,' said Kashmira bhabhi. 'We will go find him for just this one treatment.'

'Don't say things like these, Kalu, bhabhi! I feel like giving you one kaan ke neeche. First of all, you chose to make an appointment with me instead of a call. Now, you are saying all this "empty hands" and all. Are we that paraaya to you?'

'Bhabhi, don't say things like that.' Kumud bhabhi shot a sideways glance at Mansukhbhai. 'Sometimes, Manu just takes time to put his ego aside.'

'It's not the question of my ego, Kumud! Dr Garodia played with Ba's heart and health! She cried tears of blood. My mother, whom I have never seen as weak and powerless, looked lifeless for days after Dr Garodia asked for the diamond. I can't watch my mother or anybody's mother go through that again. I will feel personally responsible.' Then he pointed at Nikunj. 'Isn't he with Dr Garodia?'

'No, he is not. He is on your side here. He doesn't really want Dr Garodia back. I'm the one insisting on this.'

'Give me one good reason to bring that leech back to Mumbai, and I will do it.'

Kashmira bhabhi and Kalpeshbhai exchanged another glance, and then Kashmira bhabhi started telling Mansukhbhai about all their adventures to heal and poop. Kalpeshbhai joined the story by the time Nikunj's character was introduced. The story only ended halfway into lunch, which was served entirely in silverware with silver cutlery. Mansukhbhai didn't take a single call that he didn't need to take. The ones he took, he directed them to call his right-hand man Manojbhai instead. He told them he was busy with a family matter. Once Kashmira bhabhi and Kalpeshbhai's story finished, the rest of the lunch was eaten in silence. Then Mansukhbhai called Manojbhai and cancelled the rest of his meetings that day.

Aam ras malai (literally a rasgulla doused in aam ras) was served for dessert in large silver bowls. Mansukhbhai lapped it up, and finally leaned back in his chair and took a deep breath. Kumud bhabhi asked the servant to clear the table and bring mukhwaas. She pulled out Mansukhbhai's diabetes kit and gave him a blood sugar test. As Mansukhbhai poked himself with the needle, he looked at Kalpeshbhai and said, 'Kalu, let's give Dr Garodia one chance. I'll make the call. He'll be here in a few hours. If there is any way I can be of help to you after all these years, I will do it.'

Kumud bhabhi smiled at Mansukhbhai. 'Don't worry, I'll talk to Ba about it.' Both Mansukhbhai and Kumud bhabhi were afraid that Damuben might want to stab Dr Garodia with her own hands. (Ba later confessed to Kumud bhabhi that she would've made Dr Garodia eat the large diamond he wanted in front of her, and then watched as his innards were torn apart.) Mansukhbhai made the call to the United Colours of Daya, who were keeping watch over Dr Garodia in Baroda.

After lunch, Kumud bhabhi got one of the bedrooms in the outhouse prepared for Kalpeshbhai and Kashmira bhabhi to take a nap. Then Kumud bhabhi and Mansukhbhai retired to their own bedroom in the main bungalow. The United Colours of Daya started moving Dr Garodia. The doctor did not know why he suddenly had leverage. He instantly made a demand that his wife and son must come with him else he wouldn't be able to treat anybody. His family was the source of his energy. The United Colours of Daya called Mansukhbhai who reluctantly agreed to this demand. Dr Garodia realized the reason Mansukhbhai had called him back—somebody's faith to heal had won over Mansukhbhai's raging hatred for him. And in Dr Garodia's book, all faiths had to be manipulated for personal gain.

32

Dr Garodia and his family were choppered from Baroda to Juhu. The United Colours of Daya drove them from Pawan Hans airfield to the Patel bungalow in black SUVs—similar to the ones that drove them to Baroda. The news of his return had leaked via the house-help network. Vipulbhai, Rameshbhai, Diksha bhabhi and the Bring Dr Garodia Back movement reached the gates of the Patel bungalow to welcome him. Dr Garodia rolled down his window and took one of the garlands generously. Then he left his hand out for everyone standing in the front line to touch and get his blessings. The Dayas ensured that the car didn't stop even for a moment for him to get any traction.

Dr Garodia walked into the outhouse like he still owned it. He had that unmistakable swagger of leverage. He greeted Nikunj with a warmth that said, 'I know you don't like me, but I'm still here.' What he actually said was, 'Dikra, at least get your father inside. There he is standing outside in so much heat with Rameshbhai and other patients. Thodi toh daya kar.'

Mansukhbhai flinched at that comment but did not say anything. He didn't want to stoke Dr Garodia's ego any further. Also, everyone knew that Dr Garodia was going to try and make more demands before he treated Kalpeshbhai.

'Is he the patient?'

'Yes, I am,' Kalpeshbhai replied.

'I will need to examine you.' Dr Garodia looked at Nikunj like he was his father's son—the person who was obviously going to be his assistant in his father's absence. 'Take him to the treatment room.'

Mansukhbhai's palm started itching when Dr Garodia called the bedroom his 'treatment room'. All he wanted to do was give Dr Garodia one tight slap and get him tossed out on to the street. Nikunj's obvious reluctance to help Dr Garodia added to the tension in the room. The Mexican stand-off between Dr Garodia, Mansukhbhai and Nikunj, which held Kalpeshbhai hostage in the middle, now moved to the bedroom. Kalpeshbhai and Kashmira bhabhi were as calm as slices of cucumbers sitting on closed eyelids at a spa. Kalpeshbhai had no investment in Dr Garodia's success or failure at all. For him, the worst-case scenario was that he wouldn't poop, which would make this day like any other in his life.

Kalpeshbhai lay down on the bed, and Dr Garodia pretended to examine him from many angles like an artist looking at his model. Or a Hollywood con artist looking at the blueprint of his upcoming heist. Then Dr Garodia sent Nikunj to fetch his son along with his treatment bag. When his son was brought in with the airbag, he took the bag from his son and fished out a magnifying glass. 'Niku beta, please undress Kalpeshbhai.' Then he turned to Mansukhbhai and Kumud bhabhi. 'You two can wait outside.'

'Kalpesh, is it okay if I stay? I don't trust this man.' Mansukhbhai did not want to miss a minute of the action. He was waiting for Dr Garodia to fail, so that he could drag him by his collar out of the outhouse and beat him up in front of his patients. Kalpeshbhai didn't mind his friends waiting inside. Kumud bhabhi decided to stay with Mansukhbhai, just in case he lost it and lunged at Dr Garodia or something.

Dr Garodia scanned Kalpeshbhai's body with a magnifying glass. Everyone kept quiet. Dr Garodia broke the tension in the room by narrating everything he was doing. Apparently, he was mapping the energy lines in the body to know which points to apply muscular puncturopathy to. Apparently, all bodies have different energy lines, so there can't ever be a standard map to follow in muscular puncturopathy. This was the greatness of his craft. While allopathy treated the human body using a standard physiological model, muscular puncturopathy treated every patient uniquely.

When Dr Garodia was finally done, he looked up and said, 'I can cure him completely. Chaalta-fartaa kari daees. Just give me a few months.'

'Ae, Garodia, that's not why we have called you here.' Mansukhbhai scowled.

'We just need you to cure my constipation first,' Kalpeshbhai told the doctor.

'Of course, of course. Your energy lines definitely look cramped. I should've seen it first only. But why not get

Kalpeshbhai fully cured? It will take a few months. I can get the clinic re-opened.'

Mansukhbhai glared at him.

'I mean, I mean, not *this* clinic.' He waved around to say that he didn't mean the bungalow. 'I mean the clinic in Mulund. We can get Kalpeshbhai there whenever, no? It's for his convenience only.'

'Ae, Garodia! Wadhaare kood nai, just do what you've been brought here for.'

'I can't work when threatened like this! It would enable my healing powers more if you promised that I'll get my clinic back. It's a sacred spot where I've accumulated years of healing energy. We will need all that energy if we have to heal Kalpeshbhai.'

'Okay, okay ... Manu, calm down.' Kalpeshbhai looked at Dr Garodia, 'If you manage to make me poop, you can have your clinic back.' Suddenly, there was a massive roar from outside the bungalow. They heard Vipulbhai's voice scream, 'Dr Garodia Ki ...' The crowd responded with a resounding 'Jai!' That is when everyone realized that Dr Garodia's son was broadcasting the happenings in the room using Facebook Live ('Dr Garodia Returns' proclaimed the title grandly). Mansukhbhai snatched the phone and put it in his pocket. A loud, collective groan was heard from outside the bungalow.

Done with the distractions, Kalpeshbhai continued, 'If you don't make me poop, you go back to your Baroda house arrest tonight.'

Dr Garodia smiled. 'Okay, Kalpeshbhai, deal. Now, let's prepare for a giant shit.'

Kashmira bhabhi unpacked the portable enema kit and handed the diaper sheet to Nikunj. Mansukhbhai helped Kalpeshbhai roll from side to side as Nikunj spread the diaper sheet under him. Then they lifted his legs up and placed the bedpan under him.

Dr Garodia spotted the Maharashtra-shaped bedsore and said that he could cure that in a few sessions too. The operative words of all of Dr Garodia's diagnoses were 'just a few', or the Gujarati words for that—'thodaak aj'. He was always just a few sessions, a few days, a few months away from curing any disease he ran into.

'How many sessions will it take for you to make Kalpesh poop, Garodia?' demanded Mansukhbhai.

'I think I will give one round of treatment today and see how his body responds. Based on that, I will be able to tell how long it will take me.'

'Calculate correctly, Garodia. This is your second and last chance.'

Dr Garodia realized that this was the moment he couldn't avoid any longer. It was better to rip the bandage off than waste more time being careful about his words and actions. He diverted his attention to Kalpeshbhai's body. He poked various parts of Kalpeshbhai's flesh. Nobody said a word. He put his ear to multiple points on his body, poked those points with his fingertips. He knocked on some other points. 'Hmm. Okay. This seems to be the problem. This is fixable. Okay. Yes, I can reroute this energy from here to there. Energizing this point now. We should be done any minute now. Any minute.

Oh, wait. This has become loose. I'll have to go deeper and tighten it.' He kept moving from point to point like he was an EDM DJ live in concert and Kalpeshbhai's body was his console.

This was the first time Nikunj had seen Dr Garodia in action. This was what Vipulbhai had to watch every day for years. People were addicted to acting as DJ consoles for this maniac, Nikunj thought. Mansukhbhai was getting impatient, and nothing really was happening to Kalpeshbhai. Kashmira bhabhi and Nikunj kept their eyes fixed on Kalpeshbhai's butt. Every once in a while, Kashmira bhabhi looked up to see if Kalpeshbhai's face or eyes showed any signs of pain (beyond the pain he was already bearing as it ran through his body day in and day out). Mansukhbhai's eyes didn't leave Dr Garodia's hands. Kumud bhabhi got bored and started checking the family WhatsApp groups.

Suddenly, Dr Garodia held his finger down at one point on Kalpeshbhai's stomach and called his son. 'Beta, come here! Quickly! Hold this energy here for me. We're just about to be done.' Garodia II stepped forward and held the fort at that point. Dr Garodia moved to another point on Kalpeshbhai's waist. 'Yes, now, slowly release the energy from there. Don't worry, I'll catch it.' Garodia II slowly lifted his thumb off Kalpeshbhai's stomach. Then Dr Garodia gave him another point to press as he measured the energy levels elsewhere.

'Eureka! I found it! I found it!' He pushed a point really hard and twisted his finger on it like it was a dagger in someone's back. 'It should happen any moment now.' Everyone's eyes were on the bedpan. Everyone except Dr Garodia. He was still busy playing DJ, twisting the point of energy round and round like it was a screwdriver.

'Ahhh!' Kalpeshbhai groaned. There was a loud clang. Almost everybody jumped on hearing it, except for Nikunj and Kashmira bhabhi. Dr Garodia nearly shat his own pants. That wasn't the noise he was hoping to hear. Nikunj quickly lifted Kalpeshbhai's legs to check the bedpan. There it was, staring right back at him, the perfectly shaped golden turd, glowing with divine light. Kalpeshbhai, Kashmira bhabhi and Nikunj exchanged glances.

Mansukhbhai's jaw dropped. Kumud bhabhi's phone dropped. For a moment, Dr Garodia forgot that he shouldn't appear surprised by the results if he had to maintain his reputation. He just raised his hands in the air, and jumped up and down. And then he returned to acting as if he knew this was going to happen all along.

'No wonder something felt different about his energies. You know how our blood has haemoglobin, which has iron. His blood has auroglobin—or you can also call it sonaglobin, which is made of gold instead of iron. Gold gives out different energy radiation. It feels like small particles on the fingertips—'

'You can stop talking now,' Mansukhbhai interrupted Dr Garodia. 'And you can have your clinic in Mulund.'

Mansukhbhai called Manojbhai and asked him to lift the embargo on Dr Garodia. Manojbhai called the construction company that loaned its real estate office to Dr Garodia and got the office unlocked. 'But if I find out that you are conning someone who knows anyone I know, I will come after you again.'

'You still don't believe me, Mansukhbhai? Why can't you have faith in muscular puncturopathy therapy? I just made your friend poop a lindi made entirely of gold!' Dr Garodia went straight for the gold, just in case he got more than what he bargained for.

'Do you want me to call the security boys?'

'No, thank you. We'll find our way back.' With one foot out of the room, Dr Garodia turned around. 'Please call me if you have any more problems in the future. Kalpeshbhai, we will have our next appointment day after tomorrow.'

Dr Garodia and his family picked up their bags, and got into the black SUV they arrived in. As soon as the car rolled out of the gate, Dr Garodia popped out of the sunroof. He waved to his fans like a movie star or a politician. Vipulbhai and his friends were besides themselves, screaming, 'Dr Garodia ki Jai!'

They followed the car on foot like a rath yatra from Juhu to Mulund. On the way, the Bring Dr Garodia Back movement's team arranged for more garlands and snacks for everyone participating in the yatra. A group of people—severely ill, abled, disabled, in wheelchairs—followed Dr Garodia's car. One of the followers had even brought that giant flex portrait of the doctor from the Gholte-Butala home and propped it up on one of the cars.

Dr Garodia's victory lap got him many new followers who promised to bring their sick relatives to the clinic. They even gave their phone numbers to the Bring Dr Garodia Back club, which had now started behaving like the marketing department of his muscular puncturopathy empire. Vipulbhai got to interact with many new people and rekindle his relationship with the old picnic members. He was also happy that Dr Garodia allowed him to sit in the AC car with him for half an hour of the entire walk. In that half hour, Dr Garodia gave Vipulbhai a detailed description of how he made Kalpeshbhai poop the golden turd. When they reached the clinic a little past midnight, two of the picnic loyalists were waiting with mattresses, pillows, sheets and blankets. Still not off his miracle horse, Dr Garodia did not want to spend a moment alone. He didn't want to acknowledge the miracle and thank god, because that would mean admitting that he didn't perform the miracle. Even to himself. This was a second chance, and the only way to go was to ride the wave. So before retiring into the office and pulling the shutter down, Dr Garodia ordered his subjects to prepare a chhappan bhog for the re-opening of the clinic the next day.

33

The thing about the second golden turd that irritated Nikunj a little was that unlike with the first one, Kalpeshbhai and Kashmira bhabhi seemed happy. They did not care if the appearance of the second turd led to Kalpeshbhai being cured or not. They expected Nikunj to be happy too, but he had mixed feelings about the entire situation. Mostly because it was Dr Garodia who had made it happen. 'Let's wait and see if Dr Garodia can repeat this tomorrow,' was all he said. 'Your health depends on being able to poop regularly—not just one golden turd in months.'

The success that Dr Garodia found on his return to Mumbai was never repeated. He went to Juhu with Nikunj for a week after the big night. Each time, he returned with an empty bedpan. Kalpeshbhai and Kashmira bhabhi were not surprised. Nikunj pretended to not be surprised. He had somehow really bought into the idea of Dr Garodia being a constipation champion. The doctor made all kinds of excuses for failing—from the sun not rising at a proper angle to Kalpeshbhai having had the wrong breakfast. 'Because mustard is golden on the inside, when you use it for tadka, it blocks all the gold energy in your energy network.'

On the eighth day, Dr Garodia made an excuse to not come to Juhu. He said, 'I am feeling depleted. I will have to recharge.' Then he failed to turn up again on the tenth and the eleventh day. On the twelfth day, he made another excuse. This way, over the next few weeks, he faded out of Kalpeshbhai's life (but continued to haunt Nikunj through Vipulbhai).

The poopocalypse, which was well on its way to becoming an international phenomenon, hit Juhu next. The symptoms included a queasy stomach, which made bubbling noises, perpetual nausea and farts that smelled like they were the cause of the nausea. Mansukhbhai was one of the Patels who got affected by the gastric epidemic in its first wave. On being cured by Nikunj, he wanted to pay it forward to the community. He finally bought into the myth of Tatti Raja.

Mansukhbhai borrowed Nikunj from Kalpeshbhai and set him up at the outhouse. He invited everyone he knew, everyone he worked with, who was affected by the indigestion crisis to be treated—free of cost. After they were done with everyone in Mansukhbhai's circle, Nikunj asked if he could make the outhouse the base of his operations until the gastric storm blew over Juhu. Mansukhbhai was more than glad to help. He was a fresh convert to the religion of Tatti Raja, and wanted to prove himself. More than that, after encouraging a fraud like Dr Garodia for a while, he wanted to repay his debt to the world by supporting someone who really helped people. So he told Nikunj that all his patients would receive free treatment, courtesy the Patel family. 'This is a shibir. We will set up counters at Kalpeshbhai's family's temple also, to bring sick people here in small buses.' A large banner was put on the Patel bungalow's gate, which read: 'Paachan Tantra Shibir, 9 a.m.–9 p.m., Mofat Ilaaj.'

Mansukhbhai's overcorrection didn't help Nikunj feel less like Dr Garodia. His insecurities made him feel like he had just replaced Dr Garodia and started his own business in the outhouse. So he worked extra hard in trying to prove that he wasn't just doing it for the money.

Nikunj hadn't seen Fehmida, Buzzcut or Ghaps in all those weeks that he worked at Mansukhbhai's. He hadn't exchanged a word beyond the usual good night or good morning with Nikita. He was too exhausted by the time he returned home. The brother–sister pair would just wave at each other and watch TV till they wanted to pass out. One night, when Nikunj got home, Nikita was watching the news—if you could call it the news anymore. News channels had given up on conventional medical and scientific expertise to provide any kind of meaningful explanation for what was happening in India. They started putting pundits, babas and tantriks on the panels. What was happening was obviously some kind of prakop. Everything from corruption to the increasing freedom of women and Westernization was blamed for the epidemic playing Battle Shit with a map of India.

Nikita was in full Devdas mode that night. (She had had a quarter of rum all by herself.) She just whatsupped Nikunj with a glance and a nod. Nikunj returned the nod, and went to the bathroom to freshen up and change. When he returned, he saw that Nikita was still in Devdas mode. So he decided to start the conversation. 'Fuck, I'm so exhausted. I should still try and finish some treatments over the phone.'

'Yeah, you've been pushing yourself a bit too hard recently, haven't you?'

'I can't become like Dr Garodia.'

'I am not even going there. You deal with that insecurity on your own. I can only tell you to take it easy.'

'How can I? There are just so many patients. This takes a lot out of me.'

'Then take some help. Figure some strategy out.'

'Your help?'

'Sure? Why not? You think I can't help you with your shit? Or are you just one more man who can't take help from a woman? You don't have to be this manly man all the time. Be okay with being vulnerable.'

'What did I do … Are you sure this isn't about something else?'

'You didn't take help. You felt too high and mighty to take help from your sister.'

'Okay, tell me what you have in mind.'

'Fehmida. She's such a big social media influencer. What if you send her a voice recording of you doing your power thing? Ask her to put it out on her TikTok and Instagram.'

'I'm not sure it works that way. I have to be using my power while saying the words. Also, I don't think Fehmida will post something like this.'

'Oh, everything is about you now, isn't it? Not about the people suffering all over the country. Just take her help! Why are you so afraid of asking for help?'

'I'm not afraid to ask for help!'

'This is just like last time with jhaad phook! You have a problem asking women for help! Fehmida was willing to be vulnerable and take your help for her business meeting, wasn't she? And here you are, big Tatti Raja with his big ego.' Nikunj wasn't sure if this was one of Nikita's feminist blogosphere moments or if she was just mad at all men for something Abhimanyu did.

'I feel a part of what you are saying is not about me at all. But okay, I'll call Fehmida and ask her!'

Nikunj sent Fehmida the voice recording on WhatsApp with a message that said, 'DON'T LISTEN TO THIS!' He also called her in case she didn't read the text. He was afraid it would make her poop. And that accident sounded wrong and scary to Nikunj. When Fehmida picked up, she had already heard the voice recording. 'What is this waterfall thing?'

'You listened to it? Did something happen to you?'

'What do you mean?'

'I mean, did something happen to you in the stomach?'

'Is this your Tatti Raja thing? What is wrong with you? Why would you send it to me?'

Nikunj took a breath and then explained the plan to her.

'That sounds really, really strange,' she said, 'but if it helps people, I'll gladly help. Also, tell Didi that she is a genius for figuring this out also.'

Fehmida made a small video with the voice recording. The video was just text that said, 'Tell me if something happens to you! #CheckYourBody #StomachCrunch'. Then she posted the video on Instagram, both on her grid and as a story with the same text.

After seeing that Fehmida had posted the video, Nikunj felt proud of himself for trying something new with his powers, for trying to help people without expecting anything in return. He finally turned to Nikita and asked her, 'What's your scene? Why are you snapping?'

'Did you thank her for helping you?'

'No, I didn't feel like.'

'Good.' Nikita didn't miss a beat. 'I think Abhimanyu is going to break up with me.'

'What? Why would you think that?'

'I don't want to sound like a crazy person. So I'm not telling you.'

Nikunj didn't say anything to her. Instead, he rolled a joint and said, 'Listen, after everything that I have seen in this last one year, I don't think anything will ever sound crazy to me.'

Apparently, Abhimanyu was going through a tough time, and he ranted and snapped angrily at Nikita on WhatsApp while trying to cancel fancy dinner plans they'd made. Then he thought that she was mad at him for not taking her to dinner that evening. She tried to convince him that she wasn't insane, and then he finally broke down and told her about his worries. He was worried that he might be fired and they had just taken a small business loan to help his younger sister. Nikita listened to everything he had to say, patiently, like a good and supportive partner. 'And then he did the worst thing! He just distanced me with one sentence.'

'What did he say?'

'He said "thank you". Thanking your partner for being a partner is an act of distancing.' But obviously, she didn't want to nag him about it and get an answer right then. So instead, she chose to stew in it. She felt a lot better after narrating the story to Nikunj. On hearing the words come out of her mouth, she also realized that maybe she was attaching too much power to Abhimanyu's gratitude.

The next day, she couldn't help but snap at Abhimanyu repeatedly for tiny things. She wanted to tell him what was bothering her, but was caught somewhere between 'he will think I am crazy' and 'should I be bugging him with this right after he trusted me through a bad time?' Nikita's thirty-eighth snap of the day happened when they were driving back from work. Abhimanyu pulled the car over and asked her what was up. She broke down and told him everything. He apologized for thanking her. He said he didn't know any better. This was the first time he had talked about his feelings to anyone. And he thought thanking her was the least he could do for her tolerating his feelings. That made her laugh while drying her tears.

While Nikita had an emotional roller coaster of a day, Nikunj's day was spent following up with Fehmida for responses to her Instagram story and post. Apparently, it had been a massive failure. If it had been just a failure, it would have only failed at making people poop. But this attempt failed so hard that it became a meme. They cut out Fehmida's face and body from a screenshot of one of her older TikTok videos, put it in front of waterfalls, with the text: 'Imagine a waterfall …' Then that spiralled into words rhyming with waterfall. Fall (as in autumn), ball (as in party), aerosol Pope John Paul, Asterix the Gaul, saree ka fall. Each of them had their own images. Saree ka fall had one of Shahid Kapoor and Sonakshi Sinha from the song '*Saree ke fall sa*'. Soon the social media justice warriors got on to the meme. Words didn't need to rhyme with waterfall any more. The jokes stopped being funny after someone put a picture of a manel about women's health, and the text said, 'Imagine a patriarchy …'

Nikunj felt really bad. He sent Fehmida a long voice note apology. He was afraid that this would be the end of their relationship. She, however, sent him a boomerang where she made a face and waved his apology off. The text with the boomerang said, 'All publicity is good publicity! I got so many followers out of it!' When Nikunj apologized once again, Fehmida called him and shouted, 'You know, I am actually making a TikTok video with your audio. It's a hit! You don't understand how internet works or what?'

The good thing that came out of this experiment was that Nikunj was now driven to find an idea to reach many people at the same time. He had to prove to himself that he was better than Dr Garodia—that he was giving back many times more than the money he was making off his powers.

34

Like every superhero, Kapil Karmarkar's morning started with a close-up shot of his abs while he was in the middle of doing pull-ups. Sweat dripped from his chest to his stomach to his lifeless legs. When he was done, he finished his orange juice with a calm mind and a drive to seize the day—like a champ or a samurai. He had promised his mother that he would help her clean the loft that day. He had a counselling session with a budding Paralympic swimmer and one charity event to host, among other small duties and calls to action for the small organization he ran. So when his phone rang, he did not know that he was going to participate in a *Guinness Book of World Records* event in a few days. It was Nikunj Gholte-Butala, the young caregiving prodigy he had hired and who had become a cult figure of sorts.

Kapil Karmarkar hadn't been constipated for a long while now. He still associated Nikunj with Dhiraj, and they ran one of the best caregiving services in the city. He ended up talking to Dhiraj every now and then—also referring them to people he met. He met a lot of people, most of them disabled. He worked with them to help them unlock their true potential, get help like caregivers or assimilate through rehabilitation programmes. He had built a network of mentors and peers, and ran a WhatsApp group with one of the strictest guidelines in the country. Nikunj calling him meant that it must have been something important.

The first words Nikunj said were, 'I want to help people.'

'Hello? Nikunj?'

'Yes, it's me. And I want to help people. You are the best person I know who can help me figure this out.'

'But you are already helping a lot of people, Nikunj. Don't push yourself so hard. The problems in the world won't go away overnight. It's not a battle. It's a long war.'

'No, but I need to help more people; I need to get more organized. Can we meet for coffee?'

'You are always welcome; let's talk then. Come over to the office any time after lunch.'

Kapil Karmarkar's organization's office was in one of the smaller, failing, non-branded malls. He chose a mall because they have the best accessibility features of any commercial buildings. Plus, there are security guys and staff all the time to help in case he or any of his visitors needed assistance. A few of the shops in the mall had survived. The movie theatre stayed open because it was the only place that made money, and a lot of it. The food court was left only with non-branded food outlets—stuff that you could get on any street in Mumbai. Kapil had gotten a great deal on the failed denim store to convert it into an office. He really liked the wood and blue colours of the place, so he left the interiors intact and just added wooden desks for his team. His organization had three other people who used wheelchairs and two able-bodied interns.

Nikunj and Kapil Karmarkar sat and talked in the food court while eating Chinese bhel. Nikunj told him about the Instagram experiment. 'It worked over phone though. So there has to be a way to reach more people directly.'

'Why not try Facebook Live?'

'I think it will have the same effect as Instagram. So every time I treat someone, I have to feel a connection with them.'

'Why not try it once before eliminating the option?'

'Okay, so when do we try it?'

'Right now. I have a small Facebook page; it has some followers. Many of them are paraplegic and have regular bowel problems.'

'Let's do this.'

They found a quiet corner and tried the Facebook Live video. Sixty-eight people watched it live. Most of them sent the 'LOL emoji' because they assumed this was the organization's way of participating in the famous 'Imagine a waterfall …' meme. Needless to say, nothing happened to anybody who watched and heard that Facebook Live. Then the organization thought of assembling everyone in a big hall and giving Nikunj a mic, but that would be a logistical nightmare. No building would have that many toilets. This meant people would have to be in their own homes or with close access to a bathroom. Each group that could be treated simultaneously couldn't be more than two or three people based on how many bathrooms the host could afford.

That was when Kapil Karmarkar had a bright idea—a call chain! He pulled out the Sheaffer pen that he always had tucked in his front pocket, and drew many nodes in a line and connected them all with arrows moving in one direction. 'Each person in the call chain is responsible for merging calls with the next person in the call chain. Once everyone is online, and you connect with all of them, you can simultaneously heal so many people. It will be great publicity for my company to plan and execute this call chain!'

The two of them disbanded after finalizing on a charity call chain event. Kapil went to his office, paused work on all the other projects and got his team to start planning the execution of the biggest ever conference call in the history of telecommunication. He put out a call to action on his social media and WhatsApp, and people poured in to be a part of this historic event. They had to locate and contact as many people as they could, put them all on a shared spreadsheet to show who was going to call whom. One of the members of Kapil's Facebook group had a cousin who had a classmate who worked with the Guinness World Record authorities. That person was brought in so that the call would get coverage.

Nikunj told everyone he knew that he was going to try something big to help people. Nikita smiled like a mentor who had inspired a Nobel prize winner. Vipulbhai took the idea to Dr Garodia to see if the doctor could monetize it. Ilaben was proud of her son. Buzzcut and Ghaps found the scale of it really surprising, but they also needed to laugh because it was about poop. Fehmida warned Nikunj, 'If anything happens to you because of this hero stunt that you want to do, I will tie you to a rock and do your visarjan in the Ganpati pond.'

When Nikunj told Mansukhbhai and Kalpeshbhai about the charity call chain, they said they would be willing to sponsor the event if it meant helping so many people. Kalpeshbhai thought of this as another paitra to try in his pursuit of poop. Maybe being a part of such an event might unblock him. That was how the 'Paachan Tantra Mofat Ilaaj Call Chain Sponsored by Reva Builders & Param Churna' got the attention of the news media.

Nikunj didn't want anything to do with the news, so Kapil Karmarkar handled the press. He made sure the focus of the journalists stayed on the patients and not the person at the root of the call. He sold it as a human-interest story, not a superpower story. Mansukhbhai opened his unsold flats to people who didn't have access to a bathroom. Mansukhbhai's outhouse, once again, acted as the base of operations.

Nikunj sat on Dr Garodia's swing, surrounded by Kapil, Mansukhbhai, Kalpeshbhai and Kashmira bhabhi. One of Kapil's interns stood outside the core circle with a headset and a notepad. They had organized three chains, headed by the three remaining employees of Kapil's organization. When the chains were ready, the intern merged the three on to one call and handed the phone over to Nikunj. The process was simple. Nikunj was to announce that he had picked up the phone and ask if everyone was there. Everyone was given a number, which they had to say in order. As each number was said out loud, Nikunj connected his energy to the energy of the voice. With each connection, Nikunj imagined a shining silver thread appear out of his belly button. It split into thousands of threads—the other end of each thread was connected to a patient, waiting by or on a toilet.

When 3000 people from the epidemic-affected areas of the country were present and accounted for, Nikunj began narrating his description of a waterfall. He did a thorough job. He started by describing the wet plants as you kept getting closer to the waterfall. Then the noise. Then the first sight of the milky-white water flowing down the rocks. At various points in the call, people groaned. Everyone was advised to stay online no matter what, to maintain the chain till the end. So people left their phones on but rushed to the toilet. When Nikunj finally finished, his head started spinning and he collapsed backwards. He fell off the swing and landed on his back. He tried to get up, but the swing returned and hit him on his head.

When he woke up, he was in the main bedroom. The same circle of people who waited in the living room with him sat around the bed.

'What happened?'

'It was successful! We made 3000 people poop in one go.'

The Guinness World Record person, who was at a hotel and plugged into that call, had also responded saying he hadn't pooped like that in days. He sent in his official report calling this the longest call chain in recorded history. Of the

3000 people, Kalpeshbhai was the only person who didn't get cured.

Nikunj felt something had changed. He couldn't put a finger on it yet. Mansukhbhai hosted a celebratory dinner for Kapil and his team for executing the call chain. At dinner, Nikunj felt full and couldn't really eat much. The group started discussing the next call and how to make it bigger.

That night, Nikunj didn't stay for too long. He was exhausted from having spent all that energy, making 2999 people poop in one go. He didn't even stay up long enough to see Nikita come home. He passed out in front of the TV, playing a news channel. There was a report on the longest call chain organized by Kapil Karmarkar's organization to relieve 3000 people of the stomach problems that were doing a maut ka taandav across India.

35

The next morning, Nikunj just couldn't poop. He knew he had to, but nothing happened when he sat on the commode. He pulled his pants up and ran out of the bathroom in complete shock. He could've waited a day to be shocked, but he trusted himself as Tatti Raja to self-diagnose correctly. He needed to talk to somebody about it. He called Dhiraj first. Dhiraj asked him if he had tried using his own powers on himself. Nikunj hadn't. So he went back into the loo. He put his palms on his stomach, as if he was doing reiki on himself. He closed his eyes, and described the waterfall and the boulders. Nothing happened. He didn't even feel the power flowing out of him. Now, he thought, he had two problems: He couldn't poop and couldn't use his powers.

He called Dhiraj again and asked him to check if there were any appointments he could go for. Since he had never used them on himself before, he wanted to know if he failed because a Tatti Raja could not use his powers on himself. At that moment, Nikunj could live without pooping but not without his powers. Life would teach him otherwise very quickly, as he discovered at his first appointment that day. Dhiraj found him an elderly married couple in Thane, whose house had become a fart and burp hotbox. They refused to open their windows because old age had made them paranoid. In the middle of that, Nikunj tried to use his powers on the old man first. The old man sat in the toilet with the door unlocked but not open. Nikunj tried to connect with the old man's energy; he couldn't. So he started describing a waterfall. Nothing happened. Instead, Nikunj felt his energy dissipating into the stink-riddled room, and he collapsed on to the floor. The old lady thought he was a fraud Tatti Raja or worse, a fraud Tatti Raja who would lock them both in the bathroom and steal their belongings. So when Nikunj came to, she grabbed her hawai chappal and drove Nikunj out of the house.

Nikunj called Dhiraj and told him what happened. Dhiraj told him to try again. 'Chhote, I will find you someone more shaant than that couple. You keep patience and try your best.' This time, Dhiraj found a jolly, blind fellow, who was a teacher in Bhandup. Nikunj tried his powers with him and once again, nothing happened except Nikunj fainting. He apologized and left. He called Dhiraj, and told him to cancel all the other appointments and went home.

Dhiraj was already waiting for him at his house, drenched in sweat and anxiety. He was more sad about Nikunj losing his powers than Nikunj himself. He didn't understand how a Tatti Raja could be constipated. Nikunj didn't have anything to say that would make Dhiraj feel better.

'What will you do now?'

'I don't know ... Maybe I need to be able to relax to poop. And maybe if I pooped, I'll get my powers back.'

Dhiraj held Nikunj's hands and sat at his feet for some time. His belief systems were failing him after proving themselves to be facts of life. They sat in silence for half an hour before Dhiraj pulled out the phone he used for Tatti Raja appointments and set up an auto-answering message on it, 'We are extremely sorry for your pain. Due to unforeseen circumstances, no further appointments will be given until further notice.'

This was the first time that Nikunj understood the pain of the people he had been helping for so many months now. He realized why people were willing to threaten him or offer him large amounts of money to move their appointments up the ladder. Constipation felt like he was living the same day over and over again, no matter how different each day was. That feeling may also have partly come from him staying at home and not doing anything else with his time. He chose to stew in his constipation till Ilaben finally snapped at him one day. She said she was going to line up all possible gharelu and medical laxatives, and Nikunj was to try it day in and day out. Vipulbhai just waved his hand and said, 'I have the best solution, but when did you start listening to me in your life?' His solution was Dr Garodia, of course. Nikunj was never going to fall for that. Nikita found Nikunj's problem ironically amusing, but she still felt sad for him. She empathized with him because, as a child, she used to suffer from constipation. 'I wish we had known of your powers when we were kids,' she told him. 'All these teething problems would have gone by now. You'd have been a trained superhero.'

When Kashmira bhabhi and Kalpeshbhai called Nikunj because they hadn't heard from him in many days, he told them about his situation. That freaked them out a little bit. Kalpeshbhai was worried that he had given Nikunj his constipation by osmosis or something. He wondered if his constipation was contagious. Nikunj snapped them out of their own trip and told them he would get in touch with them once he got his powers back.

Because he couldn't focus on anything, Nikunj started helping Ilaben with her work. He did the mindless job of accompanying the rickshaw guys on their deliveries. He also went and hung out with Ghaps at the wine shop or with Buzzcut at the studio. They'd get stoned to get Nikunj's mind off his pain. This illness had really stolen any ras Nikunj had in life.

Meanwhile, at Dr Garodia's clinic, the picnic culture had died. After the brief stint at the Patel outhouse, where they were catered to by the most excellent of cooks, the picnic crowd had forgotten to feed each other. The people in the waiting area started to look like a bunch of lost lambs waiting outside a butcher's shop. When Ilaben heard about this, she decided to bring them out of the darkness. She thought that if Vipulbhai was to be involved in Dr Garodia's personal growth plan, she needed to monetize that devotion.

One Monday morning, half-way into preparing lunch orders, Ilaben told Shardaben and Toral bhabhi that she would be back in an hour. She dressed up (which meant switching to a sari from her Punjabi suit, putting on makeup and wearing her slightly high-heeled sandals) and went straight to Dr Garodia's clinic. Once she reached, she didn't bother saying hi to Vipulbhai. Instead, she went straight to Rameshbhai and asked him to add her to the clinic's WhatsApp group. Rameshbhai complied. On being added, she quickly forwarded that week's lunch and dinner menus (that Toral bhabhi had designed on Canva). Once that was done, Ilaben stood at the centre of the waiting area and announced, 'I am Ila. I am Vipulbhai's wife. Dr Garodia has been a part of our family for years now and has eaten this same food. This is a Dr Garodia–approved, *satvik*, vegetarian-only lunch and dinner service. Full, pure *Surti* thali for lunch and revolving international cuisine for dinner. Please check the menu on the WhatsApp group. Our portions are very lavish—so if you're less hungry, then two people can eat from one plate only.' On hearing this announcement, everyone jumped forward to place an order. Ilaben asked them to return to their seats, telling them that the service started from the next day and, 'Please place order with Vipulbhai, one day in advance.'

That thrilled Vipulbhai to bits, and he didn't see any grounds to rebel against his wife's move. He started to see himself as an Annadaata to that crowd of the sick, weary and hungry that gathered at the clinic–shrine–ashram of Dr Garodia. This turned out even better than bringing Mulund's famous khau galli's faafda–jalebi, where his contribution had to compete with all the other snacks that everyone else had brought. That day onwards, Vipulbhai became the sole provider of food at the clinic. His arrival and departure would start to have the same sense of importance as it did in the pre-Juhu years of the clinic.

Ilaben banked on Vipulbhai's need to be loved by everyone at the clinic, because, while she could up production easily, she would still need a separate delivery guy. In the mornings, she helped him load all the tiffins on to a rick. Someone waited at the clinic to help him off and unload all the tiffins. That was how the Gholte-Butalas started making a lot more money off Dr Garodia's cult than Vipulbhai ever had in his role as Dr Garodia's resourceful and faithful assistant.

36

Tensions ran high in Fehmida's life. She was in a game of chicken with her brother Furqan. Fehmida didn't want to tell Nikunj any of this. She felt this was her personal battle, and she had to fight it by herself. What had happened was that Furqan was sent a forward on WhatsApp. It was one of the compilations that featured Fehmida's #ColourColour challenge video. He couldn't be too sure if it was Fehmida because of the face paint. (Even though it had a TikTok @ghalatfehmida watermark in a corner.) So Furqan searched YouTube for 'ghalatfehmida' and ran into a few more compilations that featured her videos. He was a little blown. He had never inquired what she did in life. They were brother and sister for Ramzan, Eid and family functions. He knew she kept buying things online and decorating her room, but was never curious enough to find out what it was about.

One day, Furqan made the small origami colour–colour toy from his school days. When Fehmida was about to leave for the mall, he called out to her. Furqan held the small paper toy with the thumb and forefinger of each hand tucked into the slots on the underside. He then moved the toy with the rhyme, 'Colour, colour, which colour do you want?' Fehmida's eyes widened in fear. Furqan had discovered her TikTok account. She saw this as Furqan's way of threatening her to take it down without an actual confrontation. And the actual confrontation might mean telling their parents about it. So Fehmida decided to double down on her TikTok videos, especially with Nikunj.

So when Nikunj looked to Fehmida for a distraction from his constipation, Fehmida didn't need to be told twice. She already had TikTok challenges lined up—all of which needed two people being in close contact with each other. He did not want to point out how physical she was being with him because what if she stopped after he brought it up? All the time that Nikunj and Fehmida spent clinging to each other got him super thirsty, like stoned-in-Mumbai-summer thirsty—sweat-drenched-on-the-outside, but dry-cotton-on-the-inside thirsty.

They did the Titanic challenge, which, as the name suggested, needed Fehmida and Nikunj to stand with their arms spread in that iconic pose. It was shot on the corner edge of the mall's terrace with a selfie stick to make it look like they were on one end of the deck of a ship. Nikunj was constantly afraid that the camera would fall, but Fehmida was pretty confident about the shot. After the Titanic challenge, they did the #BumChums challenge. They had to sit with their butts touching and say lines from *Kuch Kuch Hota Hai*. Fehmida had to point to Nikunj's butt and mouth the line, 'But he's your best friend, yaar!' And Nikunj had to point to hers and say, 'But she's your best friend, yaar!'

Meanwhile, at home, Furqan kept making references to her TikTok videos. Once he matkaaoed his eyes from left to right to right to left while singing '*Choli ke peechhe*'. He shut up when their father shot him a look. One night when Fehmida was watching TV and he had just come home, Furqan took his plate of food and sat next to her. Fehmida kept her courage and continued sitting there, clutching the remote tightly. He turned to her and asked, 'Fehmida, who is your best friend, yaar?' She turned off the TV and went into her room.

It was the #NurseryRhymes challenge that pushed Nikunj's mardaangi over the edge. Fehmida picked '*Twinkle twinkle little star*' for the audio. For the video, she got Nikunj an XXXL-sized T-shirt with a hole in front. Then she also climbed into the oversized T-shirt with him and pushed her face out of the hole—as if her face was his belly button. Nikunj's job was to do the hand actions that went with the words. Fehmida's job was to mouth the words playing in the audio. It was the comments that got to Nikunj—comments he had learnt to ignore but couldn't in his thirsty and constipated state of mind. He had read all kinds of gaalis about 'the guy in your videos', but when he read that one of her fans offered her a space in his T-shirt too, something snapped inside Nikunj. He turned to Fehmida, grabbed her and kissed her. She jerked her face back as soon as his lips were planted on hers. She pushed his body away with a look of disappointment and disgust.

'What are you doing?'

That was the first time Nikunj raised his voice in front of Fehmida. It was more of a bark. 'What? What's wrong?' On realizing that he had just barked, he returned to his human self. 'Why don't you want to kiss me? Don't you trust me? We've spent so much time chipkoing to each other, is it too much to want to kiss the woman you love?'

Fehmida didn't reply. She packed her bag quietly and said (without hugging or touching cheeks with him), 'I'm leaving. See you soon.'

'Wait, I'll drop you.'

'No need.' She didn't look afraid that he might try to kiss her again. She just looked dejected. Something twisted inside Nikunj when he saw her expression.

To Fehmida's extremely bad luck, Furqan was in the mall atrium as she paced towards the exit. The two spotted each other and Furqan ducked behind one of the giant plants. Fehmida thought that Furqan had come to the mall to check on her. Then she got paranoid that maybe he had seen Nikunj kiss her. There was no other reason for him to duck behind the plant like that. So she ran to her room and locked it from the inside as soon as she got home. She was pretty sure that this game of chicken was going to meet its explosive end. She gathered all the courage she had, and practised telling her parents about TikTok and how she was now a legit social media influencer. She tried many variations. She wondered if she should wait for Furqan to snitch on her or if she should fire the first salvo by confessing to her parents before he did. But nothing happened that night. Realizing that she had the whole Nikunj kissing issue to deal with too, she felt her pulse and her breath rising. She decided to take a nap. She wished she had someone like Nikita in her life to advise her. She had cousins, but they were all married, so she felt like they had sold out and if she told them anything, they would definitely tell her parents. That night, when she woke up after everyone in the family went to sleep, she put streaks of black on her cheeks like it was war paint and made a video with lines from Rachel Platten's 'Fight Song' playing in the background.

Nikunj had sent her at least fifteen messages asking if they could talk. He apologized for trying to kiss her when she didn't want him to. He told her that he was an idiot. She didn't reply to any of them. At night, Nikunj saw her new TikTok, and it really pissed him off. He tried calling her, but she didn't pick up. So he called Ghaps to check if she was up. Ghaps and Buzzcut were at the godown studio working on beats and tracks. Nikunj joined them. One look at his face and both of them asked him what happened. He told them everything, starting from his constipation to Fehmida being mad at him. But Ghaps and Buzzcut only laughed. Ghaps, according to herself, was a player and had no problems making girls kiss her, even straight ones.

When Nikunj showed them the TikTok videos that Fehmida made with him, Ghaps fell silent for a moment and then erupted: 'Theoretically, your kiss has been long overdue for the time you two have been seeing each other. You spend a lot of time together, you listen, you talk, you make sure there's as much physical contact as possible, even if it is while making TikTok videos ... Maybe you didn't kiss her right. Next time, you attack, okay? You grab her by her neck or shoulder or waist and just plant a hard kiss on to her mouth. Don't force the tongue in at your first go, okay?'

Nikunj was worried that move might end their entire relationship. He wasn't ready to be left high and dry by her. Fehmida couldn't be of the type that played power games. He thought their love was innocent and beautiful. He wondered if he had seen their relationship entirely wrong.

Fehmida didn't want to stop seeing Nikunj because that would mean that she was afraid of being exposed by Furqan. She didn't want to see Nikunj because she had no headspace to process that kiss. She leaned in on self-destruction because somewhere inside her, she wanted to stop leading this double life, but she didn't have the courage to do it herself.

When Nikunj got to the mall, Fehmida was waiting for him in the atrium near one of the perfume stalls. The saleswoman had just sprayed her wrist with perfume and Fehmida sniffed it. Nikunj called out to her, she waved at him with her un-perfumed hand. She looked at his shirt but not his eyes. She spent the rest of the evening without making any eye contact with Nikunj or saying a direct word to him. Even when they ordered food, she spoke directly to the vendor and then paused for Nikunj to place his order. When they ate in silence, she looked everywhere except at Nikunj. Even when she looked at him, she looked at his chin, his sandwich, his shirt, his hands, but not his eyes. Nikunj couldn't believe that he was being punished for trying to kiss her. As constipated as he was, he didn't want to get into a fight with her, so he decided to take the punishment quietly. At least she was willing to spend time with him.

Over the next few days, when Fehmida replied to Nikunj's messages, they were only emojis or times to meet at the mall. Fehmida made quite a few mall plans with Nikunj. Once they met twice in the day—in the afternoon for a late lunch and at night for a movie. But each time, she didn't say a word to him. She had decided to push Furqan over the edge and make him snitch on her. She decided to deal with Nikunj after she survived the impending apocalypse at home.

Tired of dropping hints, Furqan cornered Fehmida on a day when nobody else was at home. Fehmida cowered at first, but then straightened her shoulders and asked, 'What?'

'I love your TikTok videos! You're such a star, Fehmida! I've been trying to tell you for a while!'

'What?! You were terrifying me! Next time, just say things; don't act so shady!'

'Your TikToks are so brilliant! Also, did you make your colour–colour video first or were you inspired by Ramolac?'

'Wait, what? I made it first. They bought it from me.'

'You made money from TikTok?!'

'Are you going to tell Ammi–Abbu?'

'No, but who is that boy in the videos?' His eyebrows popped up and down.

Fehmida changed the topic swiftly and asked him why he followed her to the mall. He said that he did not follow her. He hid when they saw each other because he was with his girlfriend, and was not ready to be 'found out' by anyone from the family yet. She laughed and told him, 'Then you should pretend you and the "friend" just ran into each other there!'

Suddenly awash with faith, Fehmida told him everything. And he, in turn, told Fehmida about his girlfriend, who was Christian, whom he had been hiding from everyone in the house. He told her he also loved eggs benedict for brunch because of the bacon bits on top. They decided that they would celebrate his upcoming birthday together at a pub. The day ended well as Fehmida now only had Nikunj to deal with. That poor lovestruck, and constipated (she thought lovingly), twit was going to be easy. There was nothing at stake here, he wasn't going to leave her.

37

On the day 'Gayatri–Utkarsha's kiss (Prod. by Buzzcut)' crossed 10K views on YouTube, Fehmida called Nikunj and said the first complete sentence to him. 'I want to celebrate the success of Buzzcut's and Gayatri's song.' Nikunj went weak in the knees when he heard her voice. 'I have already spoken to Raveena, and we will make the plan and let you know.'

Raveena, suddenly, had become a vital part of their group. She had become friends with Utkarsha when the two of them hung out at the godown where Buzzcut and Ghaps worked. She and Utkarsha even went shopping together twice. (She had invited Fehmida both times, but Fehmida had refused.) Raveena had more time than the rest of them because she worked a pure 10–6 job as a junior accountant at her father's friend's accountancy firm. She had plans of pursuing an MBA or CA, she hadn't decided yet—so she hadn't started preparing for the entrance exams. She sometimes contributed to the tracks made by Ghaps and Buzzcut by providing backup vocals. Raveena kept in touch with Fehmida through TikTok, Instagram and WhatsApp. She often made reply or mirror TikTok videos to Fehmida's. She had also tried to hang out with Fehmida alone at the mall, but Fehmida had rejected that invitation.

Fehmida wasn't used to being outside with anybody other than by herself or with Nikunj. She had vague memories of going to Juhu beach or the mall with her cousins. That stopped once they'd all grown up and gotten married. Fehmida was the youngest in a set of seven cousins on her father's side and the second-youngest on her mother's side.

So when Fehmida messaged Raveena telling her she wanted to plan a group hangout, Raveena was ready to take orders like a good soldier. The first thing that Fehmida wanted Raveena to do was to help her pick six complete outfits from the many online fashion stores. Raveena was even more kicked to learn that she was going to help Fehmida produce a TikTok video.

An oversized white shirt, an oversized black vest and black pants for Buzzcut. A white turtleneck, black jacket and black pants for Ghaps. A black skirt, black stockings and a white turtleneck, half-sleeved top for herself. A full-length black dress with spaghetti straps and a white top to wear underneath, along with black and white striped socks for Utkarsha. A white shirt, black suit (with pants and a tie) for Nikunj. And a white sleeveless top with fake metal buttons in the front and tight black pants for Raveena. Fehmida paid for all of this entirely from her TikTok earnings. She was really proud of this fact.

Fehmida and Raveena reached the mall first that afternoon. Nikunj was third, Buzzcut fourth, and Ghaps and Utkarsha came together last—and not to mention late. (Mostly because they were busy furiously making out at the studio room in the godown. Utkarsha had an off that day from work. Ghaps had called her to the godown under the pretext of making her listen to some new material. Utkarsha, obviously, knew what 'new material' was code for.)

Nikunj met Raveena and Fehmida in the mall's atrium, which usually had some products or brands on display, or some mall activity. Among activities it had had games and face-painting for kids. A couple of times, it had had a car there. Sometimes, the space was used to promote TV shows and movies with giant cut-outs, props and photo booths. That day, some TV channel was advertising their acquisition to re-run episodes of the famous '90s sitcom *Friends*. Nikunj had never watched it. He was too young, it had too much English for him to understand back when it was popular. But everyone he knew had watched the show at least a couple of times in their formative years. The TV channel had placed a fake fountain (that looked exactly like the *Friends* fountain) in the centre of the mall atrium. In front of it, was the famous couch. People took selfies and groupfies with the red, yellow and blue umbrellas and some other props from the show (like a fake Turkey with a fez and giant glasses).

Fehmida continued to treat Nikunj like she had been treating him when they were alone—without any eye contact or saying a word directly to him. Since they were not a particularly touchy–feely couple (outside of TikTok videos), nobody, not even Raveena, noticed that the two of them were acting strange. All that meant was that Nikunj was left feeling lonely in the midst of his own friends. And being alone reminded him of his constipation, and how it made him frail, sad and droopy.

They went to the same pub that they had gone to when they had all hung out together for the first time. After getting everyone decently tipsy, Fehmida said that she had an announcement to make. Raveena giggled because she already knew what it was going to be. The two of them gave everyone their outfits and told them to change. 'You are all going to be a part of my latest TikTok video.' Ghaps tried to groan, but then kept quiet when Buzzcut and Utkarsha shot her a look. Everyone changed into their given outfits and returned to their table in the bar to finish their drinks. All the outfits looked really familiar, but Nikunj couldn't remember where he had seen these before.

Everyone paused for a few seconds and looked at the *Friends* character cut-outs in the atrium and then at each other. Constipated Nikunj was going to play Ross in the video. Fehmida, dressed as Rachel, set her tripod up. She called one of the women security guards (whom she had become friends with over the last few years) to man the camera.

'I want to make the *Friends* title theme song video with all of us. At this fountain and on this couch.'

Fehmida and Raveena glared threateningly at the kids who were resting their tired and bored asses on the couch as their parents walked from shop to shop. The kids walked away grumpily. Then the gang huddled together on the sofa and watched the *Friends* intro video to memorize what actions their characters had to do. They finally shot a lot of footage of them goofing around, pretending that they were the cast of the show. Later that night, Fehmida cut the footage together and uploaded it to TikTok. The video became hugely popular. She uploaded a 'full version' to her IGTV. She didn't believe in YouTube. According to her marketing strategy, there should be no originals on YouTube. The appearance of a stolen copy on YouTube was the yardstick of success.

After that, the girls left. Raveena had to go to a cousin's birthday. Ghaps and Utkarsha went to 'catch a movie', and Fehmida went home. Once again, Fehmida refused to acknowledge Nikunj or even say bye to him. Buzzcut dropped Nikunj home. On the ride there, he asked Nikunj about his constipation, and then very cautiously asked Nikunj if something was up with Fehmida and him. Nikunj told him everything. Buzzcut just nodded and grunted to show solidarity. He said he'd ask Raveena about it. Later that night, he messaged Nikunj to tell him that according to Raveena, nothing was wrong. Fehmida told her that she wasn't mad at Nikunj at all. In fact, she told Raveena that she really loved Nikunj.

Obviously, Nikunj did not believe a word of what he said. Not because he did not trust Buzzcut or Raveena. The information just confused him because he had been giving his everything to get her attention, and she had been ignoring him completely. Buzzcut told him that according to Raveena, someone could be mad at you and still love you. 'Woh do cheezein mutually exclusive nahin hoti.'

38

Fehmida allowed Nikunj to stew in a general state of lovelessness (and constipation) till the weekend. Then on Sunday morning, she sent him an ad for the Pre-Holi Rain Dance party at the mall. 'I want to make a rain dance TikTok,' said the message with the poster. 'Meet me there.'

Loud, remixed Bollywood music was being played by a DJ, who was on the stage built in one corner of the parking lot—a part of which had been cordoned off for the rain dance party. The area was covered by a canopy of pipes with showers attached to them. Some of the showers moved to the beat of the track. The party organizers handed out aquamarine umbrellas to people entering the rain dance arena; just in case they wanted moments of shelter from the constant rain. Nikunj had collected their tickets, grabbed a couple of umbrellas and was waiting at the gate.

Fehmida's eyes didn't leave Nikunj's from the moment she got out of the rick. She had a wide grin on her face—the same grin which showed all her teeth, the one that Nikunj fell for. She was smiling like the last couple of weeks hadn't happened. Something inside Nikunj felt quenched, and he gulped once. She took advantage of his speechlessness, grabbed him by the wrist and dragged him into the showers. As she walked, the dancing crowd just made way without stopping whatever they were doing. The drops of fake rain moved in slow motion around Nikunj. So did the people who were dancing. Even the fast tempo Bollywood remix playing became a slower acoustic version. He pulled his phone out and took a picture in the format where a boy's hand is being pulled by a woman walking ahead of him. It was the first meme he ever made (and the first photo that Fehmida allowed him to keep).

When they reached the centre of the arena, she popped open her umbrella above them and stepped closer to Nikunj. She put an open palm on his chest and bent a leg upwards. Her other hand popped out of the umbrella, holding a selfie stick with her phone attached to it. Then she whispered to Nikunj, 'Follow my lead and rotate with me.' The moment they started turning, she looked deep into his eyes, and that forced Nikunj's morosely confused face into a grin. Nikunj did not know what had just happened. Then he found his mouth responding, and before he knew it, his eyes closed and he was entirely into it. The two spun in one direction. Fehmida paused the recording for a breath and some eye contact, and then the two kissed once again, this time rotating the other way. The track Fehmida used for the video was Buzzcut and Ghaps's '*Utkarsha's kiss*'.

When she stopped filming and they finally parted lips, the two of them just grinned senselessly. Nikunj felt like he had entered a dream state. His body felt the numbness he usually felt in the dream world. Despite being surrounded by water, which rained and splashed all around them, both Nikunj and Fehmida felt really hot and bothered.

As Fehmida worked the video and set it to upload, Nikunj felt a sharp pain shoot through his stomach. It was so intense that he doubled down to the floor. Fehmida shrieked and then jumped forward to ask him what was up. Nikunj breathed like a woman in labour, trying to ease the pain that crawled towards his sphincter. 'I need to go!' He got up as soon as he could breathe normally. He told Fehmida that he'd be right back and he darted straight towards the mall restroom without an umbrella.

After a sizeable dump (he had to flush twice), he walked out of the cubicle in a complete mess. His shirt buttons were open, his collar haywire, his hair pulled apart. He was exhausted. But he was many types of happy. Fehmida was smiling at him again, talking to him again and making eye contact again. Fehmida had just kissed him. He had finally pooped. And, to top it all, he was happy that he might have found another way to make Kalpeshbhai poop if there was any connection between Kalpeshbhai's constipation and his.

When Nikunj stepped out, Fehmida was waiting for him right outside (making all the other men entering and exiting the loo feel really awkward). She jumped and squealed, 'You finally pooped? Did my kiss make you poop? Did I just heal the Tatti Raja? Don't tell me if it was a false alarm. Actually, tell me if it was a false alarm, I'm sure I can take it ...'

'Fhem! Fhem! Okay, wait, listen to me! I pooped. I finally pooped! And I think I have the solution to Kalpeshbhai's problem!'

She slapped him gently. 'Idiot, at least tell me if it was the kiss that made you poop! Way to make a girl feel good about herself.'

'Yes! Yes! Something about the kiss unblocked my insides! You saved me!' Nikunj hugged her tight. She hugged him right back. Her selfie stick poked his ribs, but it didn't matter. He knew he'd survive. 'Did you know the kiss would do this to me?' he asked her hair.

'No, I just put two and two together after you grabbed your stomach and ran. Although, you know, I could just let you believe that I cured you.'

'That would backfire because then I would constantly be afraid of kissing you.'

'Who told you I wanted to kiss you after this?'

Nikunj pulled away from the hug, 'What? Was I that bad a kisser? I'm so sorry, I'll try better next time.'

Fehmida just laughed and let him believe he was a lousy kisser just because she could. He realized that he had no problem with being a bad kisser as long as Fehmida kissed him back. Then she put an arm around his elbow, and the two walked out of the mall, their clothes still drenched from the rain dance.

Nikunj dropped Fehmida home, and they kissed through the Uber ride. After that, they got on to a video call so that they could continue staring into each other's eyes. Nikunj changed into dry clothes, booked another Uber and went to Kalpeshbhai's, all while in the dreamy state of the kiss.

39

Kalpesh and Kashmira had first met at a grand wedding at Vishwakarma Baug near Vile Parle station. It was the 'in' venue for marriages and related events in the Gujarati community. They also served the best (and the purest) aam ras and undhyu, depending on the season. Kalpesh's cousin and Kashmira's best friend were getting married. The entire hall was covered in blue cloth, adorned with pink, purple and green peacocks. Even the chandelier was made of tiny glass peacocks. In the dining hall, near the mukhwaas counter, they had carved a peacock out of ice.

The moment Kashmira and Kalpesh laid eyes on each other, they knew that they belonged together, forever. This life was but a moment in their love story, which had spanned not just centuries or millennia but yugs. When they wouldn't stop finding each other's eyes across the large wedding venue, she wondered if he was a Romeo (pejoratively). A Romeo (pejoratively) was a boy who didn't miss a single blink, who kept eye contact till both of you were kissing under the gulmohar, on his bike, in prem gali. According to Dolar (Kashmira's then best friend), the only way to find out if a boy was a Romeo (pejoratively) or not was to make a face. If the boy responded positively to a sneer, he was a Romeo. If a boy withdrew upon seeing a sour face, he was a good boy. So Kashmira made a face. Kalpesh didn't expect a sneer in return for baring his heart, so he stopped looking for her. The next few times, when Kashmira's eyes went looking for his, they didn't find them. This hurt Kashmira. She felt stupid for testing her instinct with Dolar's questionable wisdom. She had started to miss peering into the depths of his eyes. She didn't know it was possible to feel like that for someone.

Kashmira took it upon herself to re-establish eye contact. She tried staring at him from various corners of the party, but either he didn't realize she was looking in his direction or he was deliberately avoiding her. It was actually the latter, but only because Kalpesh thought she was going to scold him for looking at her in a 'bad' way. So in a comic montage straight out of a Barjatya movie, she started making faces at him, chucking gende ke phool at him. He was dying to turn around and look at her once again, but he was terrified of the consequences.

Kashmira found her opportunity when the grooms' side sat down for dinner. In those days, buffet dining wasn't a thing. People sat in lines, either on the floor or on tables, and were served one after the other. At that wedding, the grooms' family was served in silver cutlery, but on the floor. Kashmira joined the serving team by grabbing a giant serving bowl of rasgullas. Kashmira leaned forward and served three people before she reached Kalpesh.

On reaching Kalpesh, she kneeled on one leg in front of him and placed the container of rasgullas on her other thigh.

Now Kalpesh had nowhere to look but at her. She squeezed all the ras out of a rasgulla and placed it in Kalpesh's rasgulla katori. He picked it up and ate it. Without the ras, it went down quickly. The two continued to stare at each other as she squeezed another rasgulla and placed it in front of him. Kalpesh started to grow more confident in this game. So with each rasgulla that went in, his face turned sweeter and sweeter till he wore a smile full of mischief. The same mischief that her eyes had filled the entire dining hall with. After fifty-odd rasgullas, Kashmira ran out of rasgullas. So she got up and walked away as if nothing had just happened. Meanwhile, all of the groom's cousins, who sat in the line after Kalpesh, gawped at the exchange, thirsting for at least one rasgulla to come their way.

Kalpesh was into two things those days—wearing white sports shoes and smoking cigarettes. Every evening, he and his friends would go to the closest paan shop in Irla and grab a smoke. Next to the paan shop was a juice centre, which was frequented by Kashmira and her friends. It was almost surprising that the two hadn't come face to face before the wedding. They recognized each other and smiled immediately. To look cool, Kalpesh took a drag of his cigarette and blew out smoke. Kashmira's smile snapped into a frown, one that hurt Kalpesh and made him cough. He tossed his last cigarette ever into the gutter and never touched one again. (He didn't know it then, but Kashmira would later make him smoke one cigarette in a failed attempt to make him poop.) Kalpesh wasn't the juice-drinking type. He preferred falooda, but you couldn't have falooda every day. So to replace his cigarette, he started fake-smoking Phantom cigarettes to give Kashmira company as she had juice with her friends.

One day, Kalpesh wrote a heartfelt letter to Kashmira and sprayed his perfume on it. In the evening, he walked over to Kashmira with one hand glued to the back of his head, nervously running his fingers through his hair, and gave her the letter. She laughed so hard when she saw that he had attached his biodata, like this was an arranged marriage proposal. She found it all very cute; so she wrote him a reply, attached her biodata and a photo of herself. She sprayed some of her perfume over it and gave it to him.

Kalpesh wanted to give Kashmira everything. He wanted to see her happy. He went and bought all the perfumes he could at the imported goods store in Irla, and used a different one for each letter. Kalpesh and his friends and Kashmira and her friends started standing together—albeit mostly quietly. Whenever they'd get bored, they'd make fun of the bespectacled boy and girl, sometimes teasing them— 'quadruple battery, octuple power'. Every time Kashmira liked the perfume Kalpesh used in a letter, she ordered a watermelon juice; else she would order a mosambi. Kalpesh got rid of all the mosambi perfume bottles by giving them away to the house staff.

This perfume bit ran so long that Kashmira made him change his perfume at their engagement. They were standing next to each other at the ceremony, and Kalpesh was wearing a new scent. Kashmira called over the waiter serving juice, and picked up the mosambi. Kalpesh immediately apologized to everyone, excused himself, went to his room, took a shower, and wore a perfume he knew she liked. When he came out, she was holding a glass of watermelon juice, giving him the same grin she had given him when serving him the rasgullas sans their ras.

The two had no innate need to rebel by announcing themselves as lovers who wanted to get married only to one another. That was the fastest way to make all the elders hate you. Even if you were of the same caste, you at least received a collective facepalm from the elders and heard murmurs rise every time you entered a room. Kashmira and Kalpesh were sure that their photos would reach them the minute their parents started looking for a good family for them. It was always a 'good family' or a 'bad family', never a 'good boy' or a 'bad boy'. Juhu parents liked to keep their daughters in Juhu, or send them to Walkeshwar or straight to the US/UK. Kalpesh and Kashmira went through the whole process of meeting and rejecting a lot of suitors until they landed on each other. They met each other under the elders' watchful eyes, and pretended to not know each other. Then they waited a week before saying 'yes'.

Their wedding was one of the biggest among the Juhu Gujaratis of their generation—beaten only by two other weddings (one of which was Mansukhbhai's). They had both aam ras and undhyu. Theirs was the first wedding in the history of the Juhu Gujarati community to serve pizza. They were also the first couple in Juhu to have a wedding music video that was shot days before the actual ceremony to the song '*Tera naam liya*' from *Ram Lakhan*. The video team had tried their best to make Kalpesh and Kashmira look like Jackie Shroff and Dimple Kapadia in the video.

Six years into their marriage, and life was beautiful. They were rich and busy. They loved each other. They were considering having a baby. They couldn't have asked for more.

Kalpesh and Kashmira had just returned from a holiday at their family's farms in Mahabaleshwar. The house help was unloading the luggage and boxes of strawberries from the car. Kashmira needed to pee so she slammed her car door shut and ran into the house. Kalpesh stepped out of the car and collapsed. His shriek echoed through the entire bungalow. When everyone gathered around him, they saw Kalpesh was on the ground, unable to move any part of his body other than his face. Pain had replaced every sensation in his body.

The last love note that Kashmira left for Kalpesh before she ran indoors was: 'Keep one box of strawberries for our room. I'll go and get that chocolate sauce that Kanukaka got from the US. We have to try that thing they did in that movie.'

That was the last time they were lovers. Since then, for twenty-two years, they had been comrades fighting the oppression of an unknown illness that had flummoxed doctors and godmen alike. Every day was a day of commiseration for an idea to poop that failed or a day of strategy to figure out how to poop next. Every moment was shaped around making sure that Kalpesh was in the least amount of pain. Their eyes had become matte black now, shallow and incomplete. The last time their eyes had lit up on seeing the other was twenty-two years ago.

So when Nikunj explained his plan to Kashmira bhabhi, he saw her eyes light up. She told Nikunj that she was going to make some arrangements, and he should get Kalpeshbhai ready. She even told him which shirt and pants he should be wearing. Nikunj went into Kalpeshbhai's room and informed him that they were going to try something new, but he wanted it to be a surprise. Kalpeshbhai, as usual, was game. Anything to poop. Nikunj found the shirt and pants that Kashmira bhabhi had mentioned and dressed Kalpeshbhai in them. He planned ahead and made sure Kalpeshbhai wore a diaper.

Meanwhile, Kashmira bhabhi managed to procure watermelon juice, mosambi juice, Phantom cigarettes, a container of rasgullas, strawberries and chocolate sauce. These were arranged on a table in the roofed Zen garden behind the house. The garden had been installed there on the advice of a Zen master, who promised to make Kalpeshbhai poop through meditation. It was complete with rocks, plants and grass flown in from Japan. It had a small waterfall and a pond filled with koi fish. The family continued to maintain the garden (even after the Zen master abandoned them) because it looked classy and beautiful. Kashmira bhabhi asked all the servants in the house to help fill the garden with candles, which flickered as they flapped loudly against the constant breeze. She set up a projector to beam their pre-wedding video on a wall.

Nikunj wheeled Kalpeshbhai into the garden to see Kashmira bhabhi rest her back against the edge of the table on which all the items of romance were placed. Kalpeshbhai smiled at first, and then tears started rolling down his cheeks. Kashmira bhabhi darted forward, cupped his face, and the two kissed. For the first time in two decades, they lost themselves in each other. Kashmira bhabhi had scripted bigger plans than to directly kiss him like that, but at that moment, she didn't care. Suddenly, Kalpeshbhai started to groan. He pushed her mouth away with his and almost screamed, 'Ow! I'm in pain! Lift me up! Lift me up!'

Both Kashmira bhabhi and Nikunj helped Kalpeshbhai up as his eyes rolled to the back of his head, and he groaned again. Except this last groan was tinged with relief. Nikunj didn't wait for him to relax completely. He pushed his hand into the back of Kalpeshbhai's pants and right into his diaper, till his fingers found something metallic and warm. He pulled out the golden turd. When he turned to show it to Kalpeshbhai and Kashmira bhabhi, they weren't anywhere to be seen. In fact, he was surrounded by a thick fog, as though someone had just turned on a fog machine. He could only see the flickering glow of the candles and the glow of the golden turd in his hand.

40

There was a sudden flash of light and the fog cleared. Nikunj was in an infinite, incandescent white space. Kalpeshbhai's wheelchair had become a throne, and Kalpeshbhai, dressed like a god from BR Chopra's *Mahabharat*, sat on it, one leg crossed over the other. Kashmira bhabhi, dressed like a goddess from the same epic TV series, was on a throne right next to him. The two of them lifted their palms up, blessing him, and smiled—a smile so benevolent that only gods, who were way past the meaning of life, were capable of.

'Thank you, Nikunj. Vishnu has forgiven us. We ask for your forgiveness if we have said or done anything to offend you.'

Nikunj hadn't heard this calm version of Kalpeshbhai's voice. 'What is this?' he gasped. 'Who are you? You are not human! What is the meaning of the three golden turds?' He wondered if Dr Garodia was right about Kalpeshbhai's blood having auroglobin instead of haemoglobin.

Kalpeshbhai got up from the throne, and started flexing and limbering up. 'Ah, I miss the use of these.' He started spot jogging.

'All this light and costume change means that our punishment is over, and now, Vishnu has forgiven us. Kalpesh laid three golden turds because Vishnu sent us to learn three truths, and now, we have learnt them.'

'You knew this backstory all along, but did not tell me?'

'No, we didn't,' Kalpeshbhai started doing lunges. 'Our memories just returned. What kind of amateur do you think Vishnu is? To punish a god and goddess, but leave their memories and powers with them? That would be no punishment at all. A god or goddess will find some jugaad to break free.'

'Or worse, they would start ruling Earth and never return to the realm of the gods,' added Kashmira bhabhi.

'Sit down, Nikunj.' A golden throne with chocolate-coloured velvety cushions appeared behind him and Nikunj sat down. 'We'll tell you everything.'

'You are the god and goddess of what exactly?'

'Of excreta.'

'I've never heard of such a god or goddess. In India, we just need an excuse to celebrate a festival or take a day off for a special pooja. I would've known about some vrat or some havan in your names.'

'Exactly! That's because we were banished from the heavens till we learned these three truths. Our existence was wiped away from human history and memory.'

'What are these three truths you keep talking about?'

'We learnt the first truth when you made me poop in a dream. We learnt the second when Dr Garodia made me poop. And just now, when we kissed, we learnt the third and last truth.'

'Tell me, Kalpeshbhai, Kashmira bhabhi, why did Vishnu punish you? What are these three truths?' Nikunj felt it was imperative to know these if he was to continue in his line of work.

'Vishnu punished us because we just had a few extra minutes of fun,' Kashmira bhabhi said. 'My real name is Kakavati and his name is Hagatarahavan—Kaks and Hags for short. We were lovers, married to each other for eternity, and we powered the excretory systems of the world—from tree sap to human poop.

'Due to our prolonged absence, the last of our powers had begun to fade from this planet. Why do you think there is a gastric storm brewing across India? The disease would slowly spread around the world and then among the animals, trees and, finally, across all realms if we didn't return to our thrones.'

'And soon, the world would be a poopy mess,' said Kalpeshbhai. 'You know how many bad decisions people take when they haven't taken a good shit? You have helped save the world, Nikunj.'

Kalpeshbhai's body jewellery clinked and clanked as he continued stretching.

'Wow! Okay.' Nikunj was doing his best to believe that he wasn't dreaming. 'Why did Vishnu punish you? Why would he put all of creation at gastric risk?'

'Buckle up, time for a flashback!' Kalpeshbhai, aka Hags, raised his hand and a control panel, which looked a lot like the buttons inside an elevator, made itself visible. He punched a button and it lit up.

'A flashback?' Nikunj was too late. Whatever that button was supposed to do had already started to happen. The incandescent white space around him faded and Nikunj found himself floating inside a NASA wallpaper of some galaxy. An ornate stone cartwheel appeared out of nowhere. Kakavati and Hagatarahavan weren't there.

Nikunj heard Kaks's voice in his ear: 'We will be the voice in your head from now on; filling you in on what you need to know about this flashback.'

'Okay ...' said Nikunj.

The stone wheel started rotating counter-clockwise with great speed. Nikunj got sucked into the wheel's vortex and re-appeared outside a grand palace. It had an army stationed outside it. With a pop, the wheel vanished and Nikunj was now inside the palace—more specifically inside what looked like a shayankaksh, or a god's bedroom.

The overall decor of the palace and the bedroom involved small turds of gold and poop emojis carved alongside the usual retro Indian design elements of peacocks, mangoes, leaves and flowers. The walls were covered with carvings and paintings of various animals, including humans pooping, peeing and sweating in different positions. It was like the Poopa Sutra, which Hags's voice confirmed. 'This is the *Ekaratni Sutra*. Ekaratni in Sanskrit is excretion.'

There was a large poop-emoji shaped bed, with big, round turd-shaped pillows. The bed was surrounded by lots of plates and bowls, all of them filled with various delicacies. There were two new sets of clothes and jewellery on two big golden thalis. There were two attendants on each side of the bed. Nikunj stopped breathing, afraid that they'd notice his presence, but then he remembered he was in a flashback and took a deep breath.

Kaks's voice rang inside Nikunj's head. 'It was Shouchotsav, the festival dedicated to us. The heavens and all the other realms celebrated Shouchotsav with great joy, seeking inner peace from a good cleanse. It was the evening of our chhappan bhog, the feast of feasts to be enjoyed after a day of cleansing your systems. As you can see, our tributes from all the realms had arrived.'

That's when Hags and Kaks burst into the shayankaksh. They looked like younger versions of Kalpeshbhai and Kashmira bhabhi. They were playful. She teased him about something. He tickled her. They kissed like Nikunj had fantasized how Fehmida and he would kiss in an empty mall after watching the last show—between breaks and giggles. Kaks pinned Hags down on to their bed, pushed aside the curtains surrounding it. She straddled him, reached for a mango from the bhog thalis and peeled it with her powers.

Hags clapped and their attendants left them alone. The two ate the mango from each side, pressing it between their mouths till it slipped and they continued kissing with their mango-filled mouths. Nikunj cringed. 'Why are you showing me this?' Hags's voice said, 'Just wait and watch!'

Suddenly, the sky above the room turned black and a bolt of lightning cracked in the sky. And again. And again.

Hags stopped kissing Kaks, looked at the sky and sighed.

Kaks grabbed his face with both her hands and made him look at her. 'Let it ring, baby! We don't have to go so quickly!'

'But we don't know who this is.' Communication technology in the realm of gods still hadn't developed caller ID systems. 'It could be any of the higher gods!'

'C'mon, how often does a higher god call upon the god and goddess of poop?' Kaks pushed Hags back down and pushed the mango against his mouth with her hand. 'And if it's a higher god, they'll understand it's for love. We have always been so diligent and perfect with our work. Plus, today is Shouchotsav! Nobody should expect anything from us today! Even if someone's calling, it might just be to wish us.'

'Yes, let's wait for once. It's just poop, right? If people aren't already cleansed because of the air, they can wait. Nobody's day is going to waste if they can't poop, right?'

Kaks's voice inside Nikunj's head provided context: 'On Shouchotsav, the air across all realms was one per cent divine laxative. It gave you the cleanse of your life—cleaning everything including the bacteria in your stomach that cause mood swings to your chakras.'

The Kaks in the bedroom returned to eating Hags's face saying, 'I'm glad we aren't gods of something more important than poop.'

Right when Nikunj was about to snap at Kaks and Hags for showing him more of them making out, Hags's voice said in his ears, 'We made the classic mistake of underestimating our responsibilities. Little did we know that we were about to piss off Vishnu!'

41

The scene in front of Nikunj cut to black. A new scene faded in. He was inside another NASA wallpaper. The wheel of time didn't show up this time. There were millions of stars and galaxies around him, all moving in different directions. He turned around to see where he was. He realized it was Vishnu's realm when he saw an empty throne made entirely out of a giant living cobra. Vishnu didn't really have a palace or anything. He seemed to have an entire realm to himself.

Nikunj heard loud groans coming from what sounded like another room, but there were no doors or pathways leading anywhere. Just the vast emptiness of space around a giant-ass cobra. Suddenly, the realm ripped open and Vishnu stormed out from another realm, one which he used as his toilet. 'I can't do this any more! Where are Hagatarahavan and Kakavati? Call them here!' He plonked his butt into the lap of the cobra.

Lakshmi followed him into the bedroom realm. 'Don't worry, darling! Everything will be alright.' She sat next to him, and ran her hand up and down his back.

'No, it won't be! Did you call Kaks and Hags?'

'Yes, I did! I left them three aakashvani messages, that too right above their bedroom! If they were there, they would've come straight to us. They must be busy with Shouchotsav, darling. Give them some time.'

'No time! No god gets to celebrate a festival when I can't even poop. Do you know what "little time" in our realm and lives means to other realms? It could be centuries somewhere else!'

Vishnu decided to make the aakashvani call himself. He summoned lightning bolts, five at a time, to call Hags and Kaks. But Hags and Kaks were eating ras malai off each other. They ignored the lightning bolts in the sky once again. Vishnu's angry face was slowly turning red with rage. 'How dare some god not pick up my aakashvani? Do they realize this could be a matter of life or apocalypse if I was calling? It's time to teach them a lesson!'

'What are you going to do now?' Lakshmi sighed. 'Not another avatar, please!'

'No avatar-shavatar! I am not going to waste time entering a human body while I'm constipated! The human might just explode because of divine pressure. It's time to teach those two a lesson. It's time to get the respect I deserve. It's time … for war.'

Vishnu's entire body burst into flames, and out of the fire rose his virat swaroop, with all his faces and hands and weapons. Lakshmi facepalmed and said, 'I'm not coming with you.'

'It's alright! I don't need you! I don't need anybody!' He stormed off. His realm faded out, and Nikunj was above

Kaks's and Hags's kingdom. A giant rip opened up in the realm and full virat Vishnu emerged. Hags and Kaks's army did not really know what to do. There was no protocol for when a higher god attacked you. So they started running helter-skelter. Vishnu eviscerated every last one of them, including the one who hid behind the giant turd statue.

The flashback followed Vishnu's path as he stormed through the palace, killing every servant or guard he ran into. Sometimes he used weapons, eye-lasers, flames shooting out of his mouth or nostrils, and sometimes he just looked at the servants and guards, and they would just drop dead.

When he finished off the last two guards and two attendants outside the bedroom, he was still in full virat mode. He stormed into the bedroom. 'WHY AREN'T YOU PICKING UP MY AAKASHVANIS?' His voice boomed and caused a small realmquake across the realms of the junior gods. (It was so terrifying that Indra and Vayu sharted in their satin dhotis.)

The poosome twosome, who were coochie-cooing while incorporating the seventeenth item on their bhog into their play, fell off the bed and spilled the Coorgi pandi curry. Before they could get on their knees and apologize, Vishnu looked at his sudarshan chakra. It fired up and started spinning like a buzzsaw designed to saw through the fabric of reality itself. Vishnu drew his hand back and aimed the chakra at Hagatarahavan and Kakavati. Kaks and Hags locked their fingers together and used their free hands to cast their powers on to Vishnu's stomach.

Thankfully, before the chakra left Vishnu's fingertip, what felt like a stone in his stomach loosened up. His eyes widened as his constipated bowels started making their way down to his colon. He lost the will to power the virat swaroop any more. The swaroop along with the chakra vanished, bringing Vishnu back to his original self.

He clutched his stomach and screamed, 'Scoundrels! Where is your loo?'

Kaks and Hags pointed him in the direction of the loo.

'You will pay for this! You will pay for this!' He screamed till he found the loo. A few seconds in, a loud 'Param Anand!' boomed across the realms of the junior gods. Golden flowers of unknown origins bloomed across the gardens of these realms, on plants that were meant for other fruits and flowers. The soldiers and servants who had lost their lives to Vishnu's full virat wrath were revived. The parts of Hags's and Kaks's kingdom and palace that were destroyed by Vishnu were put together using magical gold.

Vishnu walked out of the loo, using the satin gamchha around his neck to wipe the sweat off his brow. His mood had changed entirely. He looked happy and cheerful. Semi-naked and food-covered, Kaks and Hags fell to his feet and started to apologize 108 times. Vishnu snapped his finger and he sat on a throne that appeared out of nowhere.

'Get up, you two! You couldn't answer a simple call? It was *MY* call!'

Kaks and Hags stood with their heads bowed, like students who had been shamed in front of their entire class for not knowing the right answer.

'Also, look at yourselves! Is this how gods behave when nobody's watching? What is wrong with you two? Even Kamadev doesn't consume his *bhogs* like this!' Vishnu's mood had changed, but there was still a part of him that was angry with the two of them. 'Okay, maybe I overreacted by destroying everything that belonged to you. However, as you can see, everything has been restored.'

'Thank you, Vishnu!'

'Oh, no, no, no! There will be punishment. A junior god can't just fuck with a higher god and be let go of scot-free.'

The two of them once again fell to his feet and apologized 108 times. Vishnu let them finish this time— he fanned himself with his satin gamchha, got up, picked up one of the untouched bhogs and ate it before he returned to his seat.

'Okay, let's keep it simple. I'm cursing you to be born in the human lok. You won't remember who you are. You will go live with the humans as humans. Your existence will be wiped from all consciousness till you learn the three golden truths by which humans poop.'

Kaks and Hags looked confident. How difficult would it be for the god and goddess of poop to learn the three truths of humans poop? They would be back in their realm in no time. They touched Vishnu's feet to accept their punishment. Vishnu said, 'Tathaastu.' Kaks and Hags vanished.

That's where the flashback ended.

42

Nikunj was back in the infinite, incandescent white space. Hags and Kaks had returned to the age they were in the flashback. They were back to being the young and frolicking gods that they were.

'And now, we must go back and finish our Shouchotsav bhog ...' Hags winked at Kaks.

'Yes, yes, you can go back to your mythological kinks as soon as you explain what the three golden turds meant! What were the three truths that you learnt from them?'

'Oh, those? Those are very simple. We're surprised you haven't figured them out for yourself already.'

'I've just learnt that I've been serving gods all this while! I'm dealing with a lot right now; so if you don't mind, just tell me what these truths are.'

'So here's what everything means. The three golden turds represented the three golden truths by which humans poop.'

'At first, we lived a normal human life—' Kakavati began.

'Well, you can't exactly say normal, you two were born in rich families, easily in the top 1 per cent of over 7 billion people,' Nikunj interrupted.

'You are right,' she conceded. 'Nevertheless, we experienced a normal human life in terms of bodily functions. And then, everything was taken away from Kalpesh. All the money meant nothing. It was like we were alone in the whole universe and the universe had turned itself against us. We didn't know why it was happening to us, we were lost.'

Hags took over the narration now. 'For years, we fought, using every resource known to mankind to find a way for me to poop. Then we learnt about Tatti Raja. You became a part of our lives but our lives did not change. Then, one day, we tried lucid dreaming with you and I pooped. That was the first golden turd. It came from a dream.

'Dreams are an essential part of the human experience. Humans can dream at night and find a purpose from that dream in the day. Dreams also help you process life. You can survive your days, no matter how tough, if you're having a good time in your dreams.

'While everything can be upside-down in a dream and still make sense, the only thing that stays common between the dream world and the real world is the need to poop or pee. If you're in a dream and you need to poop or pee, you can bet your ass that you're going to wake up and run to the loo.

'So dreams were the first golden truth. That led to the first golden turd. Then came magic.'

'But jhaad phook didn't really work!' Nikunj protested.

'Because jhaad phook isn't really magic. It is just an undiscovered science.'

'Are you trying to say that Dr Garodia can actually do magic?'

'If you can do magic, then it's not really magic, is it?' Kaks reasoned.

'Nobody can do magic, Nikunj,' Hags told him gently. 'If a feat can be repeated using the same method over and over again, it's not magic. It's just science. A magical moment is unique in its provenance and being. It takes an infinite number of variables to align themselves for a magical moment to happen. Even if one of the variables is off, the magical moment won't happen. So Dr Garodia did not perform any magic, but without *his* presence that day, the magical moment wouldn't have happened.'

'So Dr Garodia has a magical quality to him?'

'When the time is right, we're all magic, Nikunj. Magic is just a moment in time that works unbelievably in your favour.' Kaks smiled.

'That was the second golden truth,' Hags continued. 'Every now and then, when we are constipated in life, we need a little magic to poop by.'

'And what was the third golden truth?'

This time, Kaks answered. 'Love. Along with dreams and magic, humans sometimes need love to poop well. We had everything—we were in love. And then Kalpesh lost his body. We forgot what it was like to express our love for each other. We didn't stop loving each other, but our fight against Kalpesh's disability made us brothers in arms. We stopped being lovers.

'We had to learn to be both. Humans sometimes spend their entire lives around each other. They dedicate their entire lives to each other. They do things for each other to show and prove their love. But they forget to express that love in and for itself. It is a very lonely feeling where you love but you only show it by doing things for the object of your love. Love is a doing verb. Sometimes you have to *do* love. Kissing Kalpesh in our human forms was us doing love, making love.

'Your experience with your girlfriend opened my eyes to it and I had to do something for Kalpesh, something to express my love, to celebrate our love. We hadn't kissed since that trip to Mahabaleshwar!'

'And now that we have experienced the three golden truths by which humans poop, our godly forms have returned,' said Hags, examining his working arms and legs in delight. 'This means Vishnu has forgiven us. It's time for us to return to our abode. I am so going to hate the smile Vishnu will welcome us back with.'

'Hags, let's just bow when we get there and wait for him to finish being smug. Let's not antagonize him for no reason. I don't want him to ruin the rest of Shouchotsav too. It's already like we're going to be celebrating Shouchotsav for the first time in a lifetime!'

'We're still better off compared to Narad! Remember when he asked Vishnu to explain maya?'

'What happened to Narad?' Nikunj couldn't help but ask.

'This was somewhere in one of the Dwapar Yugs. Younger Vishnu was a real asshole. Vishnu and Narad were out for a stroll in some forest on Earth. Narad asked him to explain the concept of maya. Vishnu asked Narad to get him a glass of water first. Then when Narad went looking for water, Vishnu made him fall in love with the first woman he saw on Earth.

Narad got married to her, raised a family and then Vishnu caused a flood in his village, destroying so many lives, including Narad's human family. Floating on a piece of wood, when Narad raged at the heavens, Vishnu replied via aakashvani, "Narad, I'm still waiting for that water. You're surrounded by so much, bring me some, na?" When a drenched, angry Narad took the glass of water for him, Vishnu said, "This is maya. You can forget what you were doing when caught in it." He wasn't even really thirsty!'

'Wow, that's really dickish.'

'Well, this kind of stuff keeps happening in the realms of gods. As they say in your realm, power corrupts and absolute power corrupts absolutely.'

It was time to say goodbye. Kaks and Hags hugged Nikunj, and returned to their realm. Nikunj was teleported to the second floor of a mall, right outside a boutique. Through the glass walls, he saw Fehmida looking at herself in the mirror, checking out the outfit she was trying on. He leaned against the railing and watched her quietly. Once she was satisfied with how she looked in the mirror, she pulled out her phone and checked herself out from various selfie angles.

She bought that dress and walked out to see Nikunj in front of her. She jumped at him and hugged him. Then she looked left, right, above, below before planting a big fat kiss on his mouth.

43

The next day, Nikunj called Dhiraj and asked him to resume setting up Tatti Raja appointments. Dhiraj was more than glad to help. The gastric storm had passed, but that didn't mean a Tatti Raja would go unemployed. There were still people who were naturally constipated. That's how Nikunj got his first appointment in weeks in Vikhroli.

Nikunj held the bedridden man's hands and started to describe a waterfall. Nothing happened. The man and his caregiver stared at him. Nikunj waited a few minutes, had a glass of water and tried again. Nothing happened. He broke into a sweat. The man's caregiver called Dhiraj and accused him of trying to con them. Nikunj apologized and left. He tried two more patients before giving up. As he waited for his Uber outside the third patient's house, he looked up and smiled at Hags and Kaks.

He took a week off to mourn and celebrate the loss of his powers, after which he joined Dhiraj in the caregiving business—back to where he had started before he became Tatti Raja.

TV reporters, who had gotten complacent because they always had the gastric storm to rely on to fill their air time, suddenly woke up and started reporting real news. There was a final investigative news report on the gastric storm on the first Sunday after the storm. The report spoke to experts from many fields, all of whom corroborated the story that the big havan that the PM of India had conducted (where he fed 1008 Brahmin pundits and 1008 cows) on live TV had driven the storm out of India and the world. Then the news channels over-corrected for their poopocalypse coverage by doing their jobs most diligently and sincerely.

Fehmida and Nikunj continued to meet at their mall. Sometimes, they were joined by Buzzcut, Ghaps, Raveena and Utkarsha. However, going for late-night shows was still something only the two of them did (mostly because they didn't tell the others. Plus, this way, they could make out all over the mall). Fehmida started making a lot of money by working branded content into her social media presence. Nikita handled all her negotiations, during which (according to Nikita) Fehmida did the job of sitting like a diva with her sunglasses on. Nikita also started using Fehmida as a consultant for content ideas to pitch to her clients.

Nikita got a big promotion and two bonuses that year alone. She was given an entire FMCG company and all its brands to handle, with a team of four working under her. She lost all her friends in the company to the bitching and backstabbing that followed. There was a company-wide rumour that she had slept with the CEO. She didn't give two fucks as long as the bosses and her team were happy. Friends were for suckers, Nikita had always said. She didn't care about making friends as long as she had Abhimanyu next to her. And she knew she had Abhimanyu. That Diwali, they told both sets of parents that they were seeing each other. The parents promptly invited each other to their respective Lakshmi pujas. They did try to seed the idea of a gol-dhaana, aka Gujarati *roka* ('for formality's sake only, beta,' they had said), but Nikita shut it down faster than a metropolitan city after a senior politician's death.

Buzzcut and Ghaps went deeper into 'artiste' territory. They booked a room for a week at that resort the three used to triple seat to. According to Ghaps, the energies of the godown studio just didn't feel right. Buzzcut's boss gave him that week off because of the success of '*Utkarsha's kiss*' in exchange for studio credit on the uploads. The next week, they released a track called '*Dekha hai pehli baar*' (predictably snapping the first half of the chorus of that song from *Saajan*) describing things in manners which went from absurd to fantastical. For example, '*Dekha hai pehli baar, Ek badak aur ek kachhua at a bar, Ek saath baara anjaano ka poora parivaar, Chaand jo tim timaaye like a big-ass star, Yaadein jo bhigaaye aankhon ko baar baar*'

'Is this like that Farhan Akhtar list song from *Rock On*?' asked Nikunj after he heard it. Ghaps promptly took his beer away for saying that. Fehmida made a TikTok using the lyrics of their song—this time even before it crossed 10K views.

Raveena started studying for her CAT exam. She knew she wanted to pursue an MBA. She nudged Utkarsha into joining her by telling her that they'd study for only one hour a day. Utkarsha, obviously, fell for it and started preparing for her CAT as well. Meanwhile, Raveena installed herself as Fehmida's friend-from-college at Fehmida's house during Eid. Fehmida had never introduced any of her friends to her family, so she did not know how to behave with Raveena around. Fehmida's mother, on the other hand, was thrilled that her daughter finally had a friend. Raveena capitalized on that emotion, and told her that there were two other girls in their gang. Her grand plan was to cook an excuse big enough so that the entire group could go to the resort for a weekend.

Ilaben, Shardaben and Toral bhabhi opened a joint savings account, and started depositing money in that account for a US trip that they dreamt of going on together. In a year, they pooled in enough money to travel to New York, eat at every authentic food joint and deconstruct their recipes to replicate them in a vegetarian format back in Mumbai. They weren't worried about having to eat non-vegetarian food in America. The trio had visited Chhotiben for that, and asked her for a solution. Chhotiben did some jhaad phook, gave them bhasm, which they put in taaveezes and wore. These taaveezes were designed to ward off evil energies from all the foreign non-veg food the women were 'going to have to' eat to learn new authentic recipes for their passion and business. Vipulbhai's life did not change much. He continued to serve and care for all the patients in Dr Garodia's waiting room.

A year later, archaeologists discovered two different sites dating back to the pre-Vedic period—one in a village in Tamil Nadu and the other in a village in Uttar Pradesh. These were old temples with carvings from the *Ekaratni*

Sutra, they housed statues of Kakavati and Hagatarahavan, and stories and scriptures that furthered Hindu mythology by adding the god and goddess of poop to the pantheon. The country's government banned public access to these temples, claiming that they went against Indian culture, and were planted by foreign invaders in the past to confuse India's future generations. The photographs and sketches of the wall carvings leaked through the interwebs—and TikTokers started making videos in which they would try the strange pooping poses prescribed in the *Poopa Sutra*.

About the Author

Jugal Mody has worked with storytelling, design and digital media across sectors from journalism to gaming. His first novel, *Toke* (HarperCollins India, 2012), was about stoners saving the world from zombies. He has also written Indian actor and star Alia Bhatt's official mobile game, *Alia Bhatt: Star Life* (Moonfrog Labs, 2017), a narrative adventure set in the Hindi film industry. Jugal was also a consulting editor with the award-winning feminist magazine *The Ladies Finger* and has collaborated on projects with comedian Aditi Mittal and online comics platform *Brainded India*.